ORLANDO

TRAVEL GUIDE

An Authentic Journey Through Orlando's Best-Kept Secrets, Iconic Landmarks, and Must-See Adventures

Valerie M. Hawthorne

ISBN: **9798282713053**

TABLE OF CONTENT

Tips for Keeping Your Valuables Safe

CONCLUSION

HOW TO USE THIS GUIDE FOR YOUR ORLANDO ADVENTURE

Imagine this: you're standing in the heart of Orlando, the sun shining down, the air buzzing with excitement, and a world of unforgettable experiences waiting just for you. The thrill of stepping into the theme parks, the joy of discovering hidden gems in the city, and the thrill of trying new foods; all these moments are just around the corner. But how do you make sure every second of your Orlando trip is as magical as it sounds?

This guide isn't just a collection of facts; it's your personal roadmap to an adventure filled with unforgettable memories. It's designed to take the stress out of planning and help you make the most of every moment. If you've ever found yourself overwhelmed by the endless options and unsure of where to start, don't worry; this guide is here to light your way.

As you read through these pages, think of me as your local friend, someone who knows all the hidden spots, the must-see attractions, and even the quiet, peaceful places where you can catch your breath amidst the excitement. I'm not just telling you where to go, I'm showing you how to experience Orlando in a way that feels like it was crafted just for you.

This isn't just about ticking off items from a list; it's about creating a journey that feels uniquely yours. Each section is filled with tips and insights that will help you plan your days, from selecting the perfect time to visit, to knowing where to stay, how to get around, and what to eat. The goal is to make your trip as seamless as possible, so you can focus on what truly matters: enjoying every single moment.

So, take a deep breath, let go of any stress, and open yourself up to the adventure that lies ahead. Whether you're visiting with family, friends, or just on your own, this guide is here to be your trusted companion, making sure that your Orlando holiday is not just a trip, but an experience that stays with you long after you return home. Trust me, you're about to embark on something truly unforgettable.

MAP OF ORLANDO

Orlando
Florida, USA

Directions

DevBerri Inc

View larger map

AC Hotel Orlando
Downtown

Jackson St

Orange
Collect

Orlando

E South St

S Rosalind Ave

City of Orlando Mayor

City Commons
Parking Garage

527

Dr. Phillips Center for
the Performing Arts

Aloft Orlando Downtown
4.3 ★ (1360)
3-star hotel

W Anderson St

Reliable Plaza

Google

Southern Gateway

SCAN THE QR CODE

1. I Recommend you use the updated/current QR Code Scanner/ App

2. Open the camera or QR code scanner app on your device.

3. Make sure the camera is facing the QR code.

4. Ensure the entire QR code is vile within the camera frame.

5. Wait for the device to recognize and scan the QR code.

6. Follow the on-screen instructions or tap the notification to access the scanned information.

INTRODUCTION

Welcome to Orlando, where the magic really comes to life. Whether you've been here before or you're about to experience it for the very first time, Orlando has this energy about it that just feels... different. There's something in the air here; call it the buzz of excitement, the promise of adventure, or maybe it's just the sun kissing your skin and the smiles all around. It's like walking into a world that's been designed to make you feel special, like it's all just waiting for you to step in and start creating memories.

I know you've probably heard all the buzz about Orlando, especially with the big-name attractions like Walt Disney World and Universal Studios. But here's the thing; there's more to this city than just theme parks. It's about the feeling you get when you're out on the lake, the rush of adrenaline from a roller coaster ride, or even just wandering down

International Drive and seeing something totally unexpected. It's the place where families come together to bond, where friends create inside jokes that last a lifetime, and where people of all ages find joy in the little things. You know, those spontaneous moments; like trying out a new restaurant you never expected to fall in love with or stumbling across an art gallery you didn't even know existed.

So, picture yourself walking through Orlando, the city that never seems to stop entertaining you. You're not just a visitor here; you're part of the magic. From the twinkling lights of Disney Springs to the serene beauty of

Lake Eola, Orlando is a place that welcomes you to both relax and have the time of your life. And it doesn't matter if you're here for the thrills or the quiet moments; this city has a way of making everyone feel at home. It's waiting for you, with all the charm and wonder you can handle.

Why Orlando is the Ultimate Holiday Destination

Alright, let's get to it: why is Orlando *the* place to be? It's a fair question, right? With so many holiday spots around the world, what makes Orlando stand out? Well, let me put it this way; there's something here for absolutely everyone, no matter your vibe, your age, or what you're hoping to get out of your vacation.

Let's start with the obvious; the theme parks. I mean, come on, you've got Disney World, Universal Studios, SeaWorld... the list goes on. These parks aren't just places to visit; they're full-on experiences. Have you ever felt your heart race as you take a ride you can't even describe? Or how about the feeling of walking down Main Street, USA, at Magic Kingdom, and realizing that this is the stuff that childhood dreams are made of? Yeah, it's that kind of place. But even if you're not into the roller coasters or the giant crowds, there's still plenty to soak up.

Orlando isn't just about big-ticket attractions. There's something charmingly *real* about this city that makes it different. I'm talking about those hidden gems, like cozy cafes where the locals hang out, or those quiet spots in the city parks that make you forget you're in the middle of a bustling metropolis. Sure, you'll find thrill-seekers diving into every ride they can, but you'll also find people relaxing by the lake, enjoying the breeze, or shopping at places you've never even heard of. It's a place where you can do it all, or absolutely nothing; and still feel like you're living the best vacation ever.

Then, there's the food. Oh, the food. From upscale dining to hole-in-the-wall gems, Orlando knows how to make your taste buds do a happy dance. Picture this: you're sitting at a trendy restaurant after a long day at the parks, sipping on a refreshing cocktail and digging into a dish that's way better than you ever imagined. It's those simple pleasures that turn a good vacation into a great one.

But honestly? The best part of Orlando is the people. You'll meet tourists from all over the world, but you'll also find that there's something about the vibe here that makes you feel like you're part of a big, happy family. The city has this unspoken charm that makes it feel like it's always been here, just waiting for you to arrive and discover it. No matter your interests, your energy, or your expectations, Orlando will show you a side of it that feels like it's made just for you.

What to Expect from This Guide

So here we are. You've picked up this guide, and you're probably wondering: What can you expect? I'm so glad you asked, because I'm excited to take you on this journey. This guide isn't just some dry list of things to do. No way. This is the inside scoop, the good stuff, the bits and pieces you can't find in every travel book. We're talking about the real Orlando; full of quirky spots, local secrets, and tips that only those in-the-know would tell you. If you're looking for cookie-cutter, generic advice, this isn't that kind of guide. We're going beyond the basics.

First, I'm going to share the best times to visit Orlando. I'll tell you when to come for perfect weather and fewer crowds, and when you might want to rethink your dates (because, trust me, it's better to know what you're walking into). The parks are amazing year-round, but there's a rhythm to Orlando's tourism seasons that can make or break your vacation. I want you to experience it all without feeling overwhelmed, and a little timing strategy goes a long way.

Next, I'll talk about where to stay. You're not just looking for a roof over your head, right? You want a place that's going to make you feel comfortable and give you that vacation vibe the second you step through the door. I'll walk you through the best hotels, the coolest resorts, and even some quirky, off-the-beaten-path accommodations that might just steal your heart.

Getting around Orlando is next on the list. This city's a bit spread out, and knowing the best way to get from point A to point B can save you time and headaches. I'll give you the inside track on public transportation, rental cars, and all the little shortcuts that make life easier. There's no need to waste precious vacation time wondering how to get to your next destination; this guide has you covered.

Of course, I'll also share the must-see attractions, but we're not stopping there. You'll get tips for experiencing them in a way that makes you feel

like you've discovered something new, even if it's your third time visiting the same park. Plus, I'll clue you in on the underrated spots; the places where the crowds are thinner, but the magic is still there. These are the hidden gems that make your trip feel personal, like you've found Orlando's soul.

By the time you're finished reading, you'll have a roadmap to the city that feels like it was made just for you. Every recommendation will be backed by real-life experiences, and every suggestion will have your best interests at heart. So, if you're looking for a guide that's more than just a list of places to go, but a conversation about how to make the most of your time in Orlando, you've found it. Ready for the adventure? Let's get started.

CHAPTER 1. PLANNING YOUR TRIP TO ORLANDO

Best Time to Visit Orlando: Weather, Events, and Peak Seasons

Alright, so you're planning your trip to Orlando, and one of the first questions on your mind is probably: When should I go? Honestly, it's a pretty crucial thing to figure out, because the timing of your visit can really make a difference in how much you get out of it.

Let's talk about the weather first. Orlando, being in Florida, is pretty much sunshine central for most of the year. But there are times when the weather can be a bit more extreme than others. The summer months, for instance; June to August; can be a bit of a heatwave. We're talking high humidity, soaring temperatures, and if you're not a fan of sweating buckets just walking to your car, you might want to think twice about coming during this time. But hey, if you're a fan of the heat and the energy of school vacations, this is when the parks are hopping. Expect long lines, packed attractions, and a crowd that's out to make the most of the summer break.

If you're looking for the perfect balance, I'd suggest aiming for spring (March to May). The weather is warm and pleasant but not unbearable, and you can enjoy all the outdoor attractions without feeling like you're melting. Plus, this time of year often coincides with some pretty amazing events. Think about spring festivals, Epcot's Flower and Garden Festival, and so many more activities that really highlight the best of Orlando. It's like the city comes alive with color, and it's just a great vibe all around.

But here's the real gem; fall. September through November is, in my opinion, one of the best times to visit Orlando. Why? For starters, the crowds thin out significantly. Kids are back in school, which means the parks are way less packed, and you can actually enjoy the attractions without feeling like you're elbowing your way through crowds. The weather is still pretty warm but not too hot, and you might even get a bit of a breeze that makes walking around much more pleasant. Plus, fall in

Orlando brings in a whole different atmosphere with Halloween festivities at the parks. If you're into the spooky season, there's no better time to get in on the action.

Winter, from December to February, is also a solid choice. The temperatures dip, so it's not quite the sunshine paradise you might be used to, but it's still relatively mild compared to northern states. The best part? The holiday decorations. Imagine walking through Magic Kingdom during Christmas time, with all the twinkling lights, parades, and seasonal magic. It's a whole different experience, and if you're in the mood for a winter escape without the freezing cold, this might be your sweet spot.

Budgeting for Your Orlando Vacation

Now, let's talk about the wallet. I know, I know, talking about money isn't the most fun part of planning a vacation, but trust me, if you get this right, it'll take a load off your shoulders and let you actually enjoy your time in Orlando without the stress of constantly checking your bank balance.

First thing's first; decide how much you're willing to spend on your trip. I'm not saying you need to make a spreadsheet or anything, but it's really helpful to set a rough budget so you don't find yourself in a tight spot later. Orlando is one of those places that can work with almost any budget. There are super affordable options if you're willing to be a little flexible, and there are luxury experiences that'll make your jaw drop if you're ready to splurge.

When it comes to theme parks, your biggest expenses will likely be tickets. But here's the trick: don't just go for the first ticket deal you find. Look for package deals or multi-day passes that can save you a bit of cash. Also, keep an eye out for any promotions, especially during the off-season. If you're planning to visit more than one park, consider going for park-hopper passes, which give you access to multiple parks in a single day. They're a bit pricier, but they're worth it if you're trying to make the most of your time.

For food, Orlando is pretty accommodating. If you're a fan of fast food or casual dining, you'll find tons of affordable places to eat, especially along International Drive. But if you're looking for a sit-down meal or something a bit fancier, the city's restaurant scene has you covered as well. Budget for at least one special meal to make your trip feel like a real treat. And don't forget about snacks! Theme park snacks can add up, so consider packing some of your own or searching for places just outside the parks where the prices aren't as inflated.

Accommodations are another place where you can adjust depending on how much you're willing to spend. There are plenty of budget-friendly hotels, motels, and even Airbnb options in Orlando. If you're willing to splurge, though, there are incredible resorts near the parks with pools, spas, and everything you need for a luxurious stay.

Where to Stay: Top Hotels, Resorts, and Unique Accommodations

So, you've booked your tickets, the excitement is building, and now it's time to think about where you'll stay. But with Orlando having so many options, how do you choose the right place that fits your vibe, your budget, and your dream vacation? Trust me, I get it. Finding the right accommodation can make or break a trip, so let's walk through the best of what Orlando has to offer; from family-friendly resorts to more unique stays that are sure to leave a lasting impression.

1. Walt Disney World Resort: The Dream Come True

If you're going to Disney World, then let me tell you; staying at one of the Disney resorts is an experience all on its own. It's like stepping into a magical world the second you check in. Now, I know this might seem a little obvious, but hear me out. Staying at a Disney resort isn't just about proximity to the parks (though that's a big plus). It's about immersing yourself in the Disney magic, even when you're not in the parks.

Take Disney's Grand Floridian Resort & Spa, for example. This place is like old-world luxury mixed with a touch of Disney charm. Think Victorian elegance meets the whimsical world of Disney; just imagine waking up to the view of Cinderella's Castle and knowing that all the

excitement of the Magic Kingdom is just a monorail ride away. Plus, the Grand Floridian is home to some fantastic dining options, like the world-renowned Victoria & Albert's restaurant. It's the kind of place that will make you feel like you're in a fairy tale, and I promise you, it's worth every penny.

But if you're traveling with the kids (or you're just a big kid at heart), you might want to look into Disney's Art of Animation Resort. It's one of the most fun Disney resorts, with rooms designed around movies like *The Little Mermaid*, *Cars*, and *Finding Nemo*. Seriously, you'll feel like you've stepped into an animated world, and the whole family will have a blast. It's not as expensive as the Grand Floridian, but it's still packed with

Disney magic. And did I mention the Big Blue Pool? It's the perfect way to cool off after a long day of park-hopping.

2. Universal Orlando Resort: Your Ultimate Theme Park Escape

Now, if you're a Universal fan, you know the power of the Wizarding World of Harry Potter. So staying at a Universal resort is kind of a no-brainer if you want the full immersive experience. Universal Orlando has some fantastic properties, like the Hard Rock Hotel and Loews Sapphire Falls Resort.

Let's start with the Hard Rock Hotel, located right next to Universal Studios. I mean, who doesn't love a little rock 'n' roll? From the moment you walk in, you're greeted with funky décor and an upbeat vibe. But it's not just about the aesthetics; staying here gets you some pretty sweet

perks, like early park admission to The Wizarding World of Harry Potter. And for the music lovers, the vibe is unbeatable. You'll feel like a rock star staying here, and honestly, who wouldn't want that?

Then there's the Loews Sapphire Falls Resort, a tropical escape right in the heart of Universal. Imagine this: swaying palm trees, a lush lagoon-style pool, and island-inspired rooms that make you feel like you're on a mini getaway in the Caribbean, but with all the perks of being right next to Universal Studios. It's one of those places where you can relax in the beautiful tropical setting and still be steps away from all the action. Plus, the resort's dining options will transport you to the islands, with places like the Strong Water Tavern serving up rum-based cocktails and Caribbean-inspired dishes. If you're looking for a more laid-back vibe but still want that Universal proximity, this place checks all the boxes.

3. The Four Seasons Resort Orlando: Ultimate Luxury

Okay, let's take it up a notch. If you're looking for the ultimate in luxury, you can't go wrong with the Four Seasons Resort Orlando. It's got everything you could possibly need for a relaxing and indulgent stay. Picture this: stunning views of the Walt Disney World Resort, a lavish spa, a championship golf course, and even a lazy river pool. The Four Seasons Orlando is known for its top-notch service, so you'll feel pampered every minute of your stay. It's also a bit more grown-up, so if you're after a quieter, more refined experience, this is the place to go.

But don't worry, it's still very much family-friendly. The kids' club is fantastic, with activities like scavenger hunts and cooking classes, so everyone in the family can have fun and unwind. And while you're living your best luxury life, your kids will be off having their own adventures in the supervised kids' program. It's like everyone gets a little slice of paradise. The Four Seasons is also just a short drive away from Disney World, so you're still close enough to all the magic without having to sacrifice the tranquil atmosphere.

4. The Wyndham Grand Orlando Resort Bonnet Creek: A More Affordable Resort with Style

Maybe you're not looking to break the bank, but you still want something a little special. Well, The Wyndham Grand Orlando Resort Bonnet Creek is an incredible option. It offers everything you'd expect from a luxurious resort but at a much more reasonable price. The resort is tucked away on 500 acres of beautiful landscape, with a serene lake and amazing views of the Disney fireworks. It's close enough to the parks for convenience but removed enough that you get a bit of peace and quiet at the end of the day.

If you're a foodie, this place won't disappoint. With dining options that range from laid-back poolside bites to gourmet meals, you'll be satisfied no matter what you're in the mood for. And the rooms? Spacious, modern, and designed for ultimate relaxation. There's also a massive outdoor pool area where you can spend hours just floating and soaking up the Florida sunshine. If you're traveling with family or a group, the Wyndham Grand offers suites that have plenty of room for everyone to spread out.

5. Airbnb and Vacation Rentals: For a Home Away from Home

Here's a thought; what if you could stay in a home rather than a hotel? Now, I know this might sound like a random suggestion, but hear me out. Orlando is home to some seriously fantastic vacation rentals that offer more space, privacy, and the kind of homey comfort you won't find in a traditional hotel. If you're traveling with a big group or just prefer the idea of having your own space, this could be your perfect solution.

Airbnb has a whole range of homes available; from cozy apartments to massive villas with private pools. Imagine staying in a beautiful home with a fully equipped kitchen, spacious living areas, and maybe even a game room to keep the kids entertained. Plus, having your own place means you can cook meals, save a bit of cash, and make your vacation feel a little more personal. Some of these vacation homes are located in prime spots, just a short drive from all the major attractions. The added bonus? You get the whole "local" feel, which can make your stay in Orlando feel like more of a real experience.

And let's not forget about those super-cool, themed vacation homes. Picture this: You and your family walk into a house that looks like it was plucked straight out of *Frozen*, or a Star Wars-themed haven. Kids will absolutely flip, and honestly, you might find yourself enjoying the novelty of it all too. It's quirky, fun, and makes your Orlando stay even more memorable.

6. The Cabins at Disney's Fort Wilderness Resort: A Bit of Adventure with Comfort

Okay, let's talk about something a little different. Have you ever thought about staying in a cabin? Not a tent or a roughing-it kind of cabin, but one that has all the comforts of home while still giving you a bit of that rustic

adventure feel? Disney's Fort Wilderness Resort offers some of the most charming cabins you'll find near the parks.

The cabins come with full kitchens, so you can cook your own meals (which is great if you're traveling with picky eaters or just want to save a bit of money). You can also rent bikes, go horseback riding, and hang out at the resort's swimming pools and recreation areas. At night, you can sit around a campfire and roast marshmallows while watching an outdoor movie. It's a lovely mix of rustic and Disney magic that feels cozy and relaxed but still very much in the heart of the Disney experience. Plus, you're just a short boat ride away from the Magic Kingdom.

Whether you're seeking luxury, fun, or something completely different, Orlando offers a wide variety of places to stay. From Disney-themed resorts to cozy vacation homes, there's truly something for everyone here. The best part? You can tailor your stay to whatever fits your style, ensuring that your trip is not just about the attractions, but about feeling comfortable, relaxed, and completely in tune with what makes Orlando so special. The next step? Just pack your bags and start your adventure; you won't regret it.

Getting Around: Transportation Tips and Tricks

Getting around Orlando is pretty easy, but knowing the best ways to move around can save you time and money, especially if it's your first time visiting. So let's break down the different options so you can get from one place to another without any hassle.

If you're sticking to the parks, you'll quickly realize that most of the big resorts offer shuttle services that take you directly to the gates. It's super convenient if you're staying on-site, but if you're not, don't worry; there are tons of other options. Taxis and ride-sharing services like Uber and Lyft are all over Orlando, making it easy to hop in and head straight to your destination. Depending on where you're staying, this can be an affordable option, especially if you're traveling in a group and can split the fare.

But here's a little tip: if you're trying to save some cash, consider using the public transportation options like the I-Ride Trolley. It's not the fastest way to get around, but it's an easy and cheap option if you're staying near International Drive and want to hit up the major attractions. Plus, it's a great way to see more of the city, at a much slower, laid-back pace.

If you're planning on exploring outside the main tourist hubs, renting a car is probably your best bet. Orlando can be a little spread out, and having a car gives you the flexibility to explore at your own pace. The drive to places like the Kennedy Space Center or the beautiful beaches on the coast can be a fun day trip, and having your own car makes it that much easier.

Navigating Orlando's Airport: Your Arrival Guide

So you've landed at Orlando International Airport, and the excitement is real. Now what? Well, first things first, the airport is pretty straightforward to get through. After you land, follow the signs to baggage claim, and if you're flying internationally, don't forget to grab your passport and get through customs.

One of the best things about Orlando's airport is that it's incredibly close to most of the major attractions. It's only about a 20-30 minute drive to Disney World or Universal Studios, so don't stress about the commute. You'll see tons of signs directing you to car rentals, shuttles, and taxis, and if you're staying at a major resort, they usually offer transport options right from the airport.

A quick tip for saving time? If you're in a rush, go ahead and grab an Uber or Lyft right from the airport. It's usually faster than waiting in the taxi line, and you can track your ride in real-time. And if you've booked a hotel or resort shuttle, make sure to check in with the transport desk to confirm your pick-up details.

Travel Essentials: What You Need to Pack

Okay, let's get down to the essentials; what to pack for Orlando. Packing for a trip can be overwhelming, but honestly, Orlando is pretty laid-back when it comes to what you need. Here's what I'd suggest:

- **Comfortable shoes**: You'll be walking a lot, and flip-flops just won't cut it. Sneakers or comfy sandals are your best friends here.
- **Sunscreen**: Trust me, you'll want to pack sunscreen, even if you're visiting in the winter months. Florida sun is no joke.
- **Water bottle**: Orlando can get hot, especially in the summer, so bring a refillable water bottle to stay hydrated throughout the day.
- **Rain gear**: Florida is known for its sudden afternoon showers, so a small, foldable umbrella or a poncho is a good idea.

- **Phone charger**: You'll be taking a ton of pictures, checking maps, and using your phone for everything, so don't forget the charger. A portable charger is a lifesaver.
- **Swimwear**: Whether you're hitting up a water park or just enjoying the resort pool, having swimwear on hand is essential.

With these essentials, you'll be all set to enjoy the adventure that Orlando has to offer. The rest? Well, that's up to you to explore. And trust me, you'll find things you didn't even know you wanted. Enjoy the ride!

CHAPTER 2. THE THEME PARKS OF ORLANDO

Walt Disney World Resort: The Magic Awaits

Okay, let's talk about Disney World. No, scratch that. Let's talk about the

experience of stepping foot into the Walt Disney World Resort, because it's not just a theme park; it's an entire world where dreams seem to come true, and magic is just around every corner. I don't care how old you are, there's something about the moment you walk down Main Street, USA, and see Cinderella's Castle that just makes your heart skip a beat. It's like the weight of the world lifts off your shoulders, and for a moment, you're a kid again. It's that simple. But the thing about Disney World is, it's not just the big-ticket attractions that make it so special. It's the feeling that, for however long you're there, you're part of something bigger.

You can't help but get swept up in the joy of it all. I mean, where else can you go to a place where everything is designed to make you smile? Where the staff; cast members, as they like to be called; greet you with a "Have a magical day!" and actually mean it? And, let's be honest, *everything* is done with such attention to detail, you can't help but be impressed. Take a minute to just look around at the parades, the street performers, or the way the park changes as the sun sets. Every corner is packed with surprises. Whether you're a first-timer or a seasoned Disney veteran, it's the kind of place that feels timeless.

And the rides? Don't even get me started. From Space Mountain to Pirates of the Caribbean, each one has its own little magic. But even the smaller, less intense rides have this charm that makes them unforgettable. There's something about Disney World that pulls you in, no matter how many times you've been there. Maybe it's the nostalgia, or maybe it's just the simple joy of being surrounded by people who are all there for the same reason: to have an amazing time. Whatever it is, it's undeniably magical.

Universal Studios Florida: Thrills and Entertainment

Now, if you're the kind of person who thrives on adrenaline, then

Universal Studios is where you'll want to head. And let me tell you, it doesn't disappoint. Universal is all about bringing your favorite movies to life, and I mean that literally. Have you ever wanted to feel like you were in the middle of a Harry Potter film? Well, you're about to get your wish. Walking through Diagon Alley and riding the Hogwarts Express to Hogsmeade isn't just something you read about in books; it's something you get to experience firsthand. That's the beauty of Universal Studios; it takes the movies you love and turns them into heart-pounding, jaw-dropping attractions that make you feel like you're part of the action.

And let's talk about the rides for a second, because Universal really knows how to turn a simple rollercoaster into an experience. Take the Incredible

Hulk Coaster, for example. If you've ever dreamed of being launched out of the gate like a rocket, this ride delivers. It's not just about the speed and the flips; it's about the whole setup, the feeling of anticipation building as you climb up and then *whoosh*; you're off and flying. The rides at Universal aren't just about thrills; they're about creating a full sensory experience that leaves you feeling like you've just stepped out of a blockbuster.

And it's not just about the action-packed rides. Universal knows how to make you laugh, too. The Simpsons Ride, the Men in Black Alien Attack; these are just as fun in their own way. It's all about variety here, and no matter what kind of theme park experience you're looking for, you'll find it at Universal. Oh, and did I mention the food? Grab a butterbeer while you're wandering through the Wizarding World; it's basically a rite of passage.

SeaWorld Orlando: An Aquatic Adventure

Now, let's take a detour from the fast-paced thrills and talk about something a little more... aquatic. SeaWorld Orlando is one of those places that really makes you appreciate the beauty of the ocean and the incredible creatures that live there. It's a completely different vibe from the big theme parks, but it's no less magical. The moment you step through the gates, you're welcomed into a world of wonder, filled with sea life that's both fascinating and beautiful.

Sure, there are rides here too, but SeaWorld really shines when it comes to animal encounters. Watching the dolphins do their thing in the shows is one of those moments that just feels *special*. And then there's Shamu. I don't care how many animal shows you've seen, there's something awe-inspiring about watching a whale leap out of the water in perfect synchronization with a team of trainers. It's pure magic, but it's also a humbling reminder of the power of nature.

But what's really cool about SeaWorld is how much you can learn while you're having fun. There's an educational side to it that makes you feel like you're walking through an interactive aquarium. From feeding rays to

learning about the rescue efforts for injured animals, there's always something new to discover. The best part? It's not just for the animal lovers out there. Even if you're not an ocean enthusiast, there's something about being surrounded by all that beauty that just makes you feel good. So, whether you're checking out the coasters like Mako or just taking in the sights of the dolphins, SeaWorld offers a peaceful, awe-inspiring experience that balances out the thrills from the other parks.

LEGOLAND Florida Resort: Fun for All Ages

If you've got little ones in tow or you're just a kid at heart, LEGOLAND Florida Resort is where the fun really comes alive. It's all about creativity, imagination, and of course, *LEGOs*. I mean, who doesn't love a giant, life-sized LEGO dragon? LEGOLAND is designed with families in mind, but don't let that fool you; it's got something for everyone. From water parks to interactive rides, this place is a whole different kind of fun.

The real magic of LEGOLAND lies in the creativity behind everything. The park is filled with colorful, detailed LEGO sculptures, and you get to experience the wonder of seeing these tiny little bricks come to life. The rides here are a lot of fun, but there's something about the interactive exhibits that really makes the place stand out. Whether you're building your own LEGO masterpiece or exploring the LEGO Kingdoms, it's all about letting your imagination run wild.

And the best part? It's not just for kids. Whether you're a LEGO enthusiast or someone who just loves seeing creativity in action, LEGOLAND has something for you. It's a park where you can feel like a kid again, no matter your age. So, whether you're riding a coaster, splashing around in the water park, or simply marveling at the incredible LEGO creations, LEGOLAND is pure fun for the whole family.

Busch Gardens Tampa Bay: A Short Drive to More Excitement

Okay, so this one's a little outside of Orlando, but it's totally worth the short drive. Busch Gardens Tampa Bay is like the grown-up cousin of the

Orlando parks; thrilling, wild, and totally packed with adventure. If you're looking for heart-stopping roller coasters, beautiful animal exhibits, and a day full of non-stop excitement, Busch Gardens is where you'll want to go.

From the moment you walk through the gates, you're greeted with lush gardens and exotic animals that make you feel like you've stepped into another world. But let's be real; the main draw here is the rides. If you've got a need for speed, then rides like SheiKra and Montu are going to blow your mind. These aren't just roller coasters; they're full-on experiences that make you feel like you're flying through the air. Plus, you've got a bunch of other thrill rides, family attractions, and shows that make Busch Gardens a place where you can spend a whole day without running out of things to do.

And don't forget the animals! Whether you're walking through the Serengeti Plain or checking out the incredible animal shows, Busch Gardens Tampa Bay is a perfect blend of thrill and nature. It's a place where you can challenge your fear on the rides and also take a moment to relax and enjoy the beauty of the world around you. It's a day trip that's worth every minute, and it's just a short drive away from Orlando.

Insider Tips for Visiting the Parks: Lines, FastPasses, and Must-See Attractions

Let's get real for a minute: theme parks can be overwhelming. The lines, the crowds, the heat; sometimes it feels like it's all a bit much. But don't worry! I've got a few insider tips that'll make your experience a whole lot smoother.

First of all, use the FastPass system. At Disney World, you can reserve rides ahead of time, which means you won't have to wait in the long lines for your favorite attractions. If you're at Universal, consider purchasing a park express pass for faster entry into some of the big rides. These little hacks can save you hours of standing in line.

Another pro tip: Get there early. Seriously, the earlier you arrive, the better. You'll be able to hit the big rides first before the lines get crazy, and trust me, the crowds grow fast. If you're visiting in the summer or during peak times, a little extra sleep won't hurt, but getting there early means you'll have a more relaxed time throughout the day.

Also, take breaks. It sounds simple, but you'd be surprised how easy it is to get caught up in the excitement. Find a shady spot or a quiet corner, grab a drink, and just chill for a bit. Trust me, it'll make the second half of the day way more enjoyable. Oh, and don't forget to hydrate! It's easy to forget in the excitement, but staying hydrated will keep you feeling good all day.

Lastly, don't miss the parades and shows! These are often the highlights of the parks and, let's face it, they offer a break from all the running around. Whether it's the fireworks show at Disney or the water-based stunts at Universal, these moments are what make the experience feel *extra special*

CHAPTER 3. EXPLORING ORLANDO'S HIDDEN GEMS

Okay, so you've probably already heard about Orlando's theme parks; the big ones, like Walt Disney World and Universal Studios. And, trust me, those places are incredible. But here's the thing: Orlando has a whole other side that most people overlook. The city isn't just about roller coasters and mouse ears; there's a whole world of hidden gems waiting to be discovered. These are the places that let you experience Orlando from a different perspective. The places that make you fall in love with the city all over again, long after you've left the theme parks behind.

Let's take a step back, take a breath, and talk about those little spots that are easy to miss if you don't know where to look. These are the quiet corners of the city, the places where you can relax, reflect, and take in the beauty that Orlando has to offer beyond the crowds. Sometimes, it's those off-the-beaten-path experiences that leave the most lasting impressions. So, let's dive into some of these hidden treasures and explore what makes them so special.

Icon Park: A New Perspective on the City

First up, let's talk about Icon Park. Have you ever wanted to get a bird's eye view of a city, just to see it from a whole new angle? Icon Park is the place for that. Situated on International Drive, this isn't your average observation wheel. It's massive, standing at a towering 400 feet. When

you step into one of the fully enclosed glass cabins, you're not just going for a ride; you're taking in the entire city; Orlando, the skyline, the theme parks in the distance, and even the nearby lakes. It's like getting a snapshot of the city, and it's jaw-dropping every single time.

The best part? It's a perfect spot for a peaceful moment to reflect and just take it all in. You're up there with no distractions, just you, the view, and the moment. It's a great way to see Orlando in a whole new light and to appreciate how much more there is to the city beyond the big attractions.

The Wizarding World of Harry Potter: Magic Beyond Universal

Okay, so, let's be real; Universal Studios has its fair share of thrilling rides and heart-pumping experiences, but nothing quite compares to stepping into The Wizarding World of Harry Potter. You might already know about the rides, the shops, and the butterbeer, but what makes this place so magical is how it makes you feel like you've actually stepped into a world of wizards and witches.

As you walk through the cobbled streets of Diagon Alley, it's hard not to get swept away by the details. The shops are straight out of the books and films, and there's something about the way the cobblestones feel beneath your feet that just takes you right into the story. It's not just a theme park experience; it's like living in a piece of the Harry Potter universe. It's one thing to see the magic on screen, but being surrounded by it; walking through the narrow alleyways, hearing the distant sound of the Hogwarts Express, and smelling the treats from the magical candy stores; is a whole new kind of spellbinding.

And, I have to tell you; if you're a Harry Potter fan, it's impossible to leave without feeling like you've been part of something bigger. It's like living a dream you never knew you had.

Gatorland: Orlando's Own "Alligator Capital of the World"

I know what you're thinking: alligators? In the middle of a theme park town? But hear me out; Gatorland is a hidden gem that's so much more than just a place to see some wild reptiles. It's got heart, personality, and a little bit of quirky charm that makes it stand out from the rest of Orlando's attractions.

Known as the "Alligator Capital of the World," Gatorland is home to thousands of alligators and crocodiles, but the experience is about way more than just looking at them through a fence. You'll get up close (but not too close!) with these incredible creatures, learning about them in ways that feel personal and exciting. You'll watch some jaw-dropping

shows where trainers interact with the alligators, and yes, if you're feeling brave, you can even try the Gatorland Screamin' Gator Zip Line, where you zip right over a pit of giant alligators below. Crazy, right?

But what makes Gatorland stand out to me isn't just the thrill of seeing these creatures; it's the way they embrace the unique nature of the park. It's a place where you can appreciate these animals in an environment that's both educational and entertaining. It's the kind of experience that leaves you with a deeper respect for the wildlife in Florida and a few fun stories to tell.

Lake Eola Park: A Relaxing Oasis in the Heart of the City

Now, let's talk about something completely different: Lake Eola Park. If you've been running around the theme parks all day, or maybe you're just looking for a quiet spot to catch your breath, Lake Eola is the perfect retreat. Situated right in the middle of downtown Orlando, this park offers a little escape from the hustle and bustle.

As soon as you step into the park, it's like the whole pace of the city slows down. There's a beautiful lake at the center, surrounded by trails, gardens, and plenty of spots to sit and unwind. You can rent a swan boat and paddle around the lake, or just relax under a tree and people-watch. It's one of those places that has a calm, peaceful energy that makes it easy to forget that you're in a major city. It's perfect for an afternoon stroll or a picnic, and it's a place where you can just let go of all the to-do lists and feel like you've found a little oasis in the middle of it all.

Kennedy Space Center: Explore the Wonders of Space

Okay, if you've ever looked up at the night sky and wondered what's out there, then the Kennedy Space Center is a must-visit. This is one of those places where the awe-factor is through the roof. You don't have to be a space geek to feel the gravity (pun intended!) of being surrounded by the history of space exploration.

As you walk through the exhibits and gaze up at the rockets, you can't help but feel like you're standing in the footsteps of astronauts who have changed the world. You'll see artifacts from the Apollo missions, get a behind-the-scenes look at NASA's ongoing work, and even have the chance to meet some of the people who made history in space. But what really gets you is the feeling that the possibilities are endless. It's a place that inspires, that makes you believe that anything is possible; and it's just an hour away from the theme parks.

The Kennedy Space Center isn't just about rockets and technology; it's about the human spirit, the drive to explore, and the wonders of what we can achieve when we look beyond the stars.

Downtown Orlando: Culture, Art, and History

You know, sometimes we get so wrapped up in the thrill of the theme parks that we forget about what's happening right here in downtown Orlando. This part of the city has its own vibe, a blend of culture, art, and history that'll make you see Orlando in a whole new light.

There's a really cool arts scene downtown, with museums and galleries showcasing local talent. The Orlando Museum of Art is a gem if you're into contemporary works, and the Charles Hosmer Morse Museum of American Art has a breathtaking collection of Tiffany glass that'll leave you in awe. But it's not just the galleries; it's the way the entire area feels like it's thriving with creativity. You can stroll through the downtown streets, exploring local shops, or grab a coffee at a cozy café and watch the city go by.

And let's not forget the history. Orlando might be famous for its theme parks, but there's so much more to this city's past than meets the eye. You can visit the historic neighborhoods, learn about the city's early settlers, or take a walk around the beautiful Lake Eola to reflect on the way this city has grown. It's the kind of place where you can stop and think about what's come before, while also looking forward to everything that's still to come.

Downtown Orlando isn't just a place to visit; it's a place to get to know, and you'll be amazed at how much there is to see if you just take the time to explore it.

CHAPTER 4. SHOPPING IN ORLANDO: RETAIL THERAPY AWAITS

So, you're in Orlando, and after a long day of theme park adventures or exploring hidden gems, the idea of some retail therapy might sound pretty tempting. Maybe you're thinking of grabbing a few souvenirs, treating yourself to something you wouldn't normally buy, or just simply wandering around some of the coolest shopping spots this city has to offer. Let me tell you, Orlando has some seriously good options when it comes to shopping; whether you're into big-name brands or you're after something unique and off the beaten path.

The best part about shopping in Orlando? It's not just about buying stuff; it's about the experience. Picture this: You're walking down a bustling street with shops on either side, the sun's shining, and you're casually window shopping but suddenly spot something you can't resist. Or, you stroll into a chic boutique, and the salesperson greets you with a smile, offering you that personal touch that makes you feel like a VIP. Orlando's shopping scene isn't just about the retail chains; it's about how it makes you feel; relaxed, excited, and completely at ease as you browse.

Let's face it; whether you're a serious shopper or someone who just likes to stroll around and people-watch, Orlando's got something to offer. You've got your ultra-modern malls, outlet centers, and a bunch of fun, quirky local shops to explore. It's the kind of place where you can make a day of it, taking your time to enjoy every little corner, every little find. And yes, while you're definitely going to see your fair share of Mickey Mouse ears and Disney tees, there's also a wealth of fashion, accessories, home goods, and unique pieces just waiting to be discovered.

International Drive: A Shopper's Paradise

Okay, so let's talk about one of the most famous spots for shopping in Orlando: International Drive, or as I like to call it, a shopper's paradise. If you haven't been to International Drive yet, well, buckle up. It's this buzzing, vibrant stretch of road that's home to some of Orlando's best shopping, dining, and entertainment. It's like Orlando in a nutshell: fun, lively, and packed with things to do, see, and buy.

International Drive is where you can truly take your time. You're surrounded by all kinds of shops, ranging from the big-name chains to local gems. If you're in the mood for some serious retail therapy, you've got everything from massive souvenir shops (hello, Disney gear!) to places that sell everything from the latest gadgets to the most stylish fashion finds. What's even better is that the shopping doesn't stop there. There are plenty of restaurants, cafes, and bars along the way, so when you get tired from shopping, you can always stop for a snack or drink and recharge.

But the real beauty of International Drive is how much it mixes up the shopping experience. One minute you could be hunting for a cute new outfit in one of the stylish boutiques, and the next minute you're browsing quirky stores that sell unique gifts and one-of-a-kind treasures you won't find anywhere else. The blend of the old and new, the high-end and affordable, makes for a shopping day that's anything but boring. I promise you, if you're not sure where to start, just pick a direction and let the shops guide you. You won't be disappointed.

The Mall at Millenia: High-End Shopping and Dining

Okay, for those of you who are looking to level up your shopping experience; let's talk about The Mall at Millenia. If you're someone who likes to indulge in a little luxury, this place is where you want to be. Think high-end, think fashion-forward, think of stepping into a world where the stores are as glamorous as the items they carry. The Mall at Millenia is Orlando's shining jewel for those who appreciate a little more luxury mixed with a lot of style.

But here's the thing: it's not just about the shopping, though the designer stores are definitely a draw. It's about the experience. The architecture of the mall itself is stunning; modern, open, airy, and packed with beautiful, high-end shops like Gucci, Louis Vuitton, Chanel, and Tiffany & Co. The kind of places where, even if you're not planning on buying a thousand-dollar handbag, it's worth walking in just to admire the displays, take in the vibes, and maybe snag a little something special that you didn't expect.

And if you're hungry after all that browsing? You're in for a treat. The Mall at Millenia offers some incredible dining options, from upscale restaurants to casual eateries that'll satisfy whatever you're craving. Imagine sitting down to a delicious meal after a successful shopping spree; feeling like you've totally treated yourself to something worthwhile. Whether it's a light bite or a full-on dinner, you'll find spots that cater to all kinds of tastes. And don't forget to stop by one of their cozy cafés for that post-shopping pick-me-up.

Even if you're not in the mood for a shopping spree, it's still worth visiting just for the vibe. The Mall at Millenia offers something a little more refined, a little more luxurious, and a little more elevated than your average mall. You don't have to buy anything; just enjoy the ambiance and let yourself get caught up in the allure.

Disney Springs: Shopping with a Side of Magic

Okay, here's the thing about Disney Springs: It's not just shopping, it's an experience. Seriously, it's one of those places where, if you're not careful, you'll end up spending hours just soaking it all in. If you've been to Disney World, you've probably heard of it, but if you haven't, get ready. This is where shopping meets magic in a way that only Disney can pull off.

First of all, Disney Springs is huge. It's this sprawling, open-air shopping, dining, and entertainment district that feels like a mini-vacation all on its own. The shops here are just a little bit extra, and I mean that in the best way possible. You've got everything from classic Disney merchandise to high-end boutiques and unique artisan stores. I'm talking about exclusive collections you can't get anywhere else; things that scream "I was here, and I found something you won't believe!"

But honestly, the best part? The atmosphere. There's just something about walking around Disney Springs. It's full of life, with live music, entertainment, and the gorgeous waterfront views that make you feel like you're on vacation even if you're just shopping. You can grab a snack from one of the many vendors, take in a performance, or simply sit back and watch the world go by. If you love the idea of shopping but also want to enjoy the experience; this is the place for you.

The stores here are a blend of Disney magic and some seriously cool brands. If you're a Disney fan (and let's be real, who isn't?), you can find some amazing limited-edition items, and if you're after something a bit more upscale, there are plenty of trendy stores to check out. All in all, it's shopping with a sprinkle of pixie dust, and I think we can all agree that it's pretty magical.

Orlando International Premium Outlets: Discounted Deals

Okay, let's switch gears and talk about deals; because who doesn't love scoring a bargain while shopping, right? If you're looking for discount shopping with top-notch brands, Orlando International Premium Outlets is your go-to spot. This place is an absolute goldmine for anyone who loves a good deal but doesn't want to compromise on quality.

The best part about the Premium Outlets is that you get the big-name brands at a fraction of the price. You'll find stores like Nike, Coach, Michael Kors, and Kate Spade offering discounts that are sometimes too good to pass up. It's like the ultimate shopping treasure hunt; where you're hunting for deals, and every store is full of treasures waiting to be found. You'll feel that rush of excitement when you walk out of a store knowing you just scored something amazing at a price that's almost unbelievable.

But here's the kicker: It's not just about the deals; it's about the experience of hunting for them. As you walk around, you can feel the energy. The Premium Outlets is designed to make shopping feel like an event. There's a sense of excitement in the air, like you're part of an exclusive club of savvy shoppers who know where to find the best deals. So, if you're the type who loves scoring a bargain and taking home a haul, this place will definitely be a highlight of your Orlando shopping adventure.

Local Boutiques and Unique Finds: Supporting Small Businesses

Now, for those of you who are into something a little more offbeat; Orlando has a treasure trove of local boutiques and one-of-a-kind shops just waiting to be explored. This isn't the mass-produced stuff you'll find in chain stores. I'm talking about local artists, makers, and small-business owners who pour their heart and soul into their work. And trust me, there's something truly special about finding that perfect, handmade item that's totally unique to the city.

The great thing about shopping local in Orlando is that you're not just picking up something to remember your trip by; you're supporting the community. You're getting a piece of Orlando that's authentic, quirky, and full of personality. From artisanal jewelry to hand-poured candles and original artwork, you'll find plenty of cool, meaningful things that'll make your trip feel even more memorable.

So, whether you're hitting up an art gallery, browsing through a vintage clothing shop, or picking up something made by a local artisan, these smaller, independent stores will give you a shopping experience that feels personal and unique. And who knows? You might just find something that's perfect for you; or for a gift you'll be excited to give.

That's the magic of Orlando's shopping scene. No matter what you're looking for, there's something that'll catch your eye and make your trip feel complete. From the big malls to the hidden local gems, Orlando has a way of turning shopping into an experience; a memory in the making. Happy shopping, my friend!

CHAPTER 5. DINING IN ORLANDO: A CULINARY JOURNEY

Alright, let's talk about food. I mean, what's a trip to Orlando without indulging in some seriously good eats, right? Trust me when I say, Orlando is a food lover's dream. From casual bites to luxurious feasts, this city has it all, and every meal can turn into a mini adventure of its own. Whether you're craving comfort food after a long day in the parks or looking for a culinary experience that'll make you feel like a true connoisseur, Orlando's food scene has something just for you.

The best part? Orlando is one of those cities where every meal is an opportunity to explore. You're not just eating to fill your stomach (although that's definitely part of it), but you're tasting a piece of the city itself. Every dish, every bite, tells a story about this place, its culture, and its people.

So, let's dive into what makes dining in Orlando such a fun, flavorful experience. I'll take you through the best spots, from hidden gems to famous destinations, and give you a peek into the kinds of flavors you can expect. Let me tell you, this city doesn't hold back when it comes to food.

Top Restaurants for a Taste of Florida

When you're in Florida, you need to try Florida. And no, I don't mean just the beach or the theme parks; I'm talking about the food that represents the heart and soul of this sunshine state. You know what I mean, right? Fresh seafood, tropical fruits, and those distinctive flavors that scream "Florida."

Let's start with a classic, **The Ravenous Pig**. It's one of those spots that's not only popular with the locals but a must-try for anyone visiting the city. Located in Winter Park, this gastropub blends modern takes on

classic Florida fare. Think slow-roasted meats, charcuterie boards, and decadent house-made pastas. The vibe? It's sophisticated but not stuffy; perfect for a laid-back yet elevated dining experience. I'm telling you, if you're looking for that perfect mix of casual yet special, this place will hit the spot.

Then there's **Victoria & Albert's** at Disney's Grand Floridian Resort. If you're here for an unforgettable dining experience, this is the place. It's a Michelin-starred restaurant, so expect impeccable service and dishes that taste as good as they look. Whether you're in the mood for a multi-course meal or just a dessert that feels like it's straight out of a fairy tale, Victoria & Albert's will show you a side of Orlando that's just as magical as its parks.

Of course, there are tons of places to grab some fresh seafood too; think **The Boathouse** at Disney Springs. Located right on the water, this restaurant serves up some of the best seafood you'll ever have. Fresh oysters, shrimp, and fish are just the start, but it's the laid-back vibe and beautiful waterfront view that make this spot truly unforgettable. Whether you're sitting on the patio or inside, it's the kind of place that'll make you feel like you've just discovered your new favorite hideaway in the city.

Dining with a View: Best Outdoor and Waterfront Spots

Now, let's talk about those meals that come with a side of scenery. There's something about enjoying a delicious meal while overlooking beautiful views that makes the experience feel... well, a bit more special, don't you think?

If you're in the mood for something a little more scenic, **The Orlando Eye** is definitely the spot to hit. It's one of those places where you can enjoy a meal while also taking in stunning views of the city. You can't beat the experience of eating while you're high above the city, gazing out at the skyline, and watching the sun set. It's both a restaurant and an experience wrapped into one, and believe me, you'll want to bring your camera along for the ride.

And if you love waterfront dining (who doesn't, right?), head over to **Lake Nona's Canvas Restaurant & Market**. This place offers great food and even better views of Lake Nona. It's the perfect spot to have dinner with friends or family, enjoy some craft cocktails, and watch the boats go by. The modern menu features fresh ingredients and creative spins on classic dishes, making it the kind of place where you'll want to linger long after the sun dips below the horizon.

But, oh, there's one more spot you can't miss; **Café Tu Tu Tango**. Not only does it have the funky, artsy vibe that will make you feel like you're in a cozy little secret spot, but it's also right by the lake. The small-plates menu is perfect for sharing, and the colorful setting just adds to the magic of enjoying some tapas-style dishes in a lively atmosphere.

Theme Park Dining: What to Eat Inside the Parks

You didn't think I'd forget the theme park food, did you? Let's face it; while the rides and attractions might be the main event in the parks, the food is definitely an experience in itself. And Orlando does theme park food in a way that's both fun and mouthwatering.

Let's talk about **Disney World** first. Now, when most people think of theme park food, they think of the usual quick bites; hot dogs, pretzels, and maybe a turkey leg or two. But Disney is a whole different ballgame when it comes to dining. **Be Our Guest** in Magic Kingdom is an experience that goes beyond food. Imagine dining inside the Beast's castle, surrounded by opulent rooms and a menu that's nothing short of exquisite. French-inspired dishes, delicious steaks, and decadent desserts; it's like you're part of the magic.

If you're in **Epcot**, you're in for a treat. Seriously, there's so much variety here, it's like taking a world tour without ever leaving the park. Have you ever had **fish and chips** in the UK Pavilion? What about fresh sushi in Japan? Or maybe you're craving a quick bite of the famous **Cronut** from France. Epcot's World Showcase is a food lover's dream come true, and you can get a little taste of every corner of the globe without needing a passport.

Then there's **Universal Studios**, where the food isn't just theme park grub, it's actual dining experiences. One of the best spots is **The Three Broomsticks** in Harry Potter World. If you're a fan of the Wizarding World, you've got to try the iconic **Butterbeer** (don't worry, it's non-alcoholic) and a plate of **fish and chips** that'll have you feeling like you're dining at Hogwarts. Oh, and let's not forget the **Lard Lad Donut**; it's as big as your face and just as delicious as it sounds.

International Cuisine: Savor the World in Orlando

What I love about Orlando is how it's not just a city, it's a world in itself. And when it comes to food, it brings global flavors right to your plate. In every corner of this city, you can taste dishes from all over the world.

For a taste of **Italy**, head to **Vincenzo's** in Winter Park. This little gem serves up homemade pasta that tastes like it's straight from Nonna's kitchen. It's one of those places that makes you feel like you've stepped into an authentic Italian eatery, and trust me, you'll want to order the entire menu.

In the mood for something a little more exotic? Head over to **Morimoto Asia** at Disney Springs for a fusion of Japanese flavors with a twist. It's not just sushi here; it's an experience. The menu is filled with unique dishes that'll make your mouth water just reading it. Think about having **Peking duck** served with the crispy perfection that only a master chef can create.

If you're craving **Mexican** food, I can't recommend **Café Tu Tu Tango** enough. The margaritas are cold, the tacos are loaded, and the vibe is so lively that you'll feel like you've stumbled upon a hidden spot in a Mexican town. It's got this funky, artsy vibe with a menu that's both delicious and fun.

Family-Friendly Dining Spots: Where to Eat with Kids

Traveling with kids? Orlando's got your back when it comes to dining spots that are perfect for the whole family. **T-Rex Café** at Disney Springs is like something out of a kid's dream. You're dining in a prehistoric world, surrounded by giant dinosaurs and immersive environments. But don't worry, it's not just the atmosphere that's great. The food is solid too, with fun dishes like **Jurassic chicken tenders** and **dino-shaped pizza** that the kids will go wild for.

If you're looking for something a little quieter, but still family-friendly, head over to **The Polite Pig**. It's casual, it's cozy, and it's got some seriously good barbecue. The kids will love the **pulled pork** sandwiches, and the adults can dive into some craft beer while enjoying the laid-back, Southern-style vibe.

Nightlife and Bars: The Best Places to Unwind After Dark

Alright, let's switch gears for a second. After a long day of exploring the parks, sometimes you just need to wind down, right? And what better way to do that than with a refreshing drink in hand? Orlando's nightlife scen

is just as vibrant as the rest of the city, and there are plenty of spots to enjoy a drink, meet new people, or just relax after the excitement of the day.

One of the coolest places to check out is **The Edison** at Disney Springs. It's a bar, restaurant, and entertainment venue all rolled into one. Picture this: you walk in and feel like you've stepped into a 1920s speakeasy, complete with live music, vintage cocktails, and a fun atmosphere that never gets old. It's the perfect mix of relaxation and excitement.

And if you're into craft cocktails, you can't miss **The Courtesy** in downtown Orlando. This place is a hidden gem, offering expertly crafted drinks in a chic, intimate setting. The bartenders here are serious about their craft, and you'll love trying something new and unique.

Orlando may be known for its theme parks, but its culinary scene is just as much of an adventure. There's something for everyone, no matter what you're craving or what kind of experience you're looking for. So go ahead, eat your way through the city, and make every meal part of the adventure!

CHAPTER 6. FAMILY FUN: ACTIVITIES FOR ALL AGES

Discovery Cove: Swim with Dolphins and Enjoy Nature

If you've ever dreamed of swimming with dolphins, let me tell you; Discovery Cove is where that dream comes true. Imagine this: you're floating in crystal-clear water, the sun beaming down, and suddenly, a friendly dolphin glides past you with a graceful flick of its tail. It's like stepping into a dream, but it's all real. And what makes it even better is that you're not just observing the dolphins from a distance; you're right there with them, experiencing it all firsthand.

Discovery Cove is not your typical theme park. It's more like an exclusive tropical oasis, tucked away in Orlando, and it's got a vibe that's completely different from the hustle and bustle of other attractions. When you step inside, you're greeted by a serene, beachy atmosphere that immediately sets the tone for relaxation and wonder. You can swim in the freshwater lagoon, snorkel through coral reefs, and even wade through a lazy river surrounded by lush greenery. It's the kind of place where you can disconnect from everything and just enjoy the beauty of nature.

But the real star of the show? The dolphins. The park offers a signature Dolphin Swim experience, where you get to interact with these intelligent creatures in a way that's incredibly personal. You'll get up close, swim with them, and even get a chance to hug and kiss them (yes, it's as magical as it sounds). They're gentle, curious, and totally playful, and it's hard to put into words just how special it feels to be in the water with them. It's a bonding moment, almost like you're connecting with a piece of the ocean's soul. And I've got to say; it's one of those experiences that will stay with you forever.

Beyond the dolphins, there's so much more to explore. The park has several habitats filled with exotic birds, rays, and tropical fish. You can spend time in the aviary, hand-feeding colorful birds or just marveling at their beauty as they fly around you. If you're a fan of wildlife and nature, you're going to fall in love with this place. And the best part? It's all about preserving nature and protecting these incredible creatures, so you're not just having fun; you're learning and connecting with the world around you.

If you're visiting with family, this is a great place to go. It's relaxing enough for adults to enjoy, but it's also thrilling and magical for kids. You can all come together for a once-in-a-lifetime experience and leave with memories that will last long after you've dried off. It's an adventure that's both heartwarming and humbling; a perfect way to bond and reconnect with nature as a family.

Crayola Experience: Colorful Fun for Kids

Alright, let's talk about a place that's *all* about color, creativity, and fun; Crayola Experience. If you have kids with you, this is a stop you absolutely cannot miss. You know how sometimes you walk into a place and it just feels *magical*? Crayola Experience is one of those places. It's like stepping into a world where everything is

brighter, more playful, and filled with endless possibilities.

This interactive experience is all about letting kids (and honestly, adults too) tap into their creativity. You'll find a ton of hands-on activities where you can color, draw, create, and just get totally immersed in the Crayola magic. Whether you're a kid who loves to color inside the lines or someone who prefers to let their imagination run wild, there's something here for everyone. It's an experience that feels like playtime on steroids; full of fun, laughter, and endless entertainment.

One of the coolest parts is the Crayon Factory, where you can actually watch how Crayola crayons are made. It's super educational, but done in such a fun way that you won't even realize you're learning. Kids love the interactive stations, where they can melt crayons down into cool shapes or design their own Crayola crayon labels. And if you're a fan of digital fun, there are stations where you can digitally color pictures or even make your own animated creations. It's an entire world of color and creativity, and you might just find yourself getting caught up in the excitement too.

It's also an ideal spot if you're looking to give your kids a chance to be hands-on and let their imaginations run wild. Kids can create their own art, take it home with them, and even send their creations to a virtual art gallery. It's a place where they can feel like real artists, and that sense of accomplishment and pride will stay with them long after you've left. It's perfect for families, but really, it's a fantastic spot for anyone who enjoys a little bit of whimsy and creativity.

So, if you're looking for something that will keep the little ones entertained, let them unleash their creativity, and make you smile at the same time, Crayola Experience should be on your list. It's a spot that combines fun, learning, and a splash of color, and it's bound to be a highlight of your Orlando trip.

The Escape Game Orlando: Solve Puzzles and Build Memories

If you've ever wanted to test your wits, work with your friends or family, and feel the adrenaline rush of solving a mystery, The Escape Game Orlando is the place to be. It's one of those activities that feels like an adventure; without leaving the room. You and your team are locked in a themed room, and your mission? To figure out clues, solve puzzles, and escape before time runs out.

What's so great about The Escape Game is that it's not just about finding hidden keys or trying to figure out combinations. It's about teamwork, communication, and having a blast while you're at it. Whether you're working through a mystery, navigating a prison break, or trying to escape a spy mission, you'll feel completely immersed in the experience. The rooms are designed to make you feel like you're part of a story, and they really know how to build tension and excitement.

It's perfect for groups; whether you're traveling with friends, family, or even coworkers. Everyone has a role to play, and it's one of those rare experiences where you can work together and feel that sense of camaraderie when you figure something out. And if you don't escape? Well, you'll laugh about it and probably want to come back and try again.

The Escape Game Orlando has different themed rooms, so you can choose the one that appeals to you the most. Some of them are more intense, others are a bit lighter, but all of them are a lot of fun. It's an activity that brings people together and creates memories that will make you smile every time you talk about them. Plus, there's something incredibly satisfying about figuring out the final clue and making your escape. It's like your very own movie moment.

So, if you're looking for something a little different and a whole lot of fun, The Escape Game is a must. It'll get you thinking, laughing, and working together; and it's an experience you won't forget.

WonderWorks: Interactive Fun for the Entire Family

WonderWorks is one of those places that you'll walk into, look around, and say, "Wow, this is unlike anything I've seen before." It's a giant upside-down building, which alone is enough to get your attention. But once you step inside, it's a world of fun, excitement, and interactive exhibits that make you feel like you're part of the adventure.

The beauty of WonderWorks is that it has something for everyone. Kids will love the hands-on exhibits, while adults can enjoy the cool science experiments and technology-driven activities. From simulating the feeling of being in a hurricane to testing your strength on a bed of nails, WonderWorks is all about pushing the boundaries of your imagination. It's a place where learning meets fun, and every corner has something that's both educational and entertaining.

One of the highlights? The Laser Tag arena. It's the perfect way to burn off some energy while having a blast. And if you're looking for something a little more chill, the indoor ropes course lets you climb, swing, and conquer your fears at your own pace. WonderWorks makes science and learning fun; it's interactive in the best way possible, and you're bound to leave with a sense of accomplishment and maybe even a few new things learned.

It's one of those spots that makes you feel like a kid again, where you can forget about the world outside and just have fun with the people you're with. Whether you're in the mood for some mind-bending science or just want to have some silly fun, WonderWorks delivers.

Fun Spot America: Go-Karts, Roller Coasters, and More

Okay, if you're in Orlando and you haven't checked out Fun Spot America, what are you waiting for? This place is a roller coaster enthusiast's dream, with all the thrills you could ask for. From heart-pounding rides to classic arcade games, Fun Spot America has that perfect balance of nostalgia and excitement.

It's also the kind of place where you can just let loose and feel like a kid again. The go-karts are a blast; you'll find yourself racing your family or friends around the track, trying to get the fastest time. And if that's not enough, there are roller coasters that will leave you grinning from ear to ear. The Skycoaster is particularly crazy; it's a giant swing that launches you 300 feet in the air, and if that doesn't get your heart racing, I don't know what will.

But here's the thing: Fun Spot America is all about fun, and that's what makes it such a great spot for families. It's not just about the big thrills; though there are plenty of those. It's also about the simple joy of playing games, riding rides together, and enjoying the classic carnival atmosphere.

So, if you're after a place where the whole family can have a blast, Fun Spot America is the way to go. There's something for everyone, from the littlest ones to the adults who are still kids at heart.

CHAPTER 7. NATURE AND OUTDOORS: THE NATURAL BEAUTY OF ORLANDO

Wekiwa Springs State Park: Explore Florida's Natural Springs

Let's talk about something that might surprise you about Orlando; the natural beauty. Sure, the theme parks are world-famous, but there's this whole side to the city that many people overlook. You know, the kind of place where you can really breathe, where the air smells like fresh pine trees, and the only sound you hear is the rustle of leaves and birdsong. One of my absolute favorite places to experience this is Wekiwa Springs

State Park. If you're even a tiny bit into nature, this place will steal your heart.

Wekiwa Springs is just about a 30-minute drive from downtown Orlando, and let me tell you, it's worth every minute. When you pull into the park, you'll immediately feel the pace of your day slow down. It's like stepping into a different world. You're greeted by crystal-clear waters that flow out of the springs at a constant temperature of around 72 degrees year-round. It's always refreshing, and the best part? The springs are fed by an underground aquifer that's been around for thousands of years. Imagine standing there, knowing that the water you're wading through has been traveling deep underground before making its way to the surface. How cool is that?

If you're a fan of swimming or tubing, you'll love the spring-fed river. The water is so clear, you can see all the way to the bottom, where schools of fish dart around. If you're not into getting in the water (no judgment, I get it!), you can still enjoy the park's hiking trails. The park has miles of trails that wind through forests, offering up beautiful views of the lush surroundings. You'll spot wildlife; deer, wild turkeys, maybe even an alligator or two, though don't worry, they're typically pretty shy and stay out of your way.

There's something incredibly peaceful about just being there. You'll find yourself completely absorbed in the beauty around you. There's a certain stillness in the air, the kind that's hard to describe unless you experience it for yourself. If you want to get away from the fast-paced theme park life for a little while, this is your escape. Plus, the park has camping grounds, so you can truly immerse yourself in nature if you're up for it. Just think; falling asleep under a blanket of stars, with the sound of crickets and distant frogs to lull you to sleep. It's magical.

Harry P. Leu Gardens: Stunning Gardens in the City

Alright, let's switch gears a bit. If you're more into peace and beauty than full-on outdoor adventure, Harry P. Leu Gardens is the perfect place to slow down and take in nature's art. Located just a few minutes north of downtown Orlando, this 50-acre garden is a true gem, and it's one of those places you visit and think, "Wow, how did I not know this existed?"

The gardens are absolutely gorgeous; no matter when you go, there's always something in bloom. In fact, there are several themed gardens here, each with its own personality. You've got the rose garden, which feels like it's straight out of a fairytale, with its lush roses in every shade

you can imagine. Then there's the butterfly garden, which, as the name suggests, is filled with flowers that attract all kinds of fluttering creatures. Honestly, it's like stepping into a real-life Pinterest board.

But what really makes Leu Gardens special is the way it makes you feel. I've walked through it during all kinds of seasons, and no matter the time of year, it always feels peaceful and refreshing. You'll find little nooks to sit in, where you can just soak in the beauty and let the stress of everyday life slip away. There's this kind of serenity that wraps around you as you walk through the gardens. You'll pass giant palm trees, a historic house at the center of the gardens, and rows of plants you might never have seen before. It's one of those places where you can just get lost in the moment, breathing in the fresh air and taking it all in.

One of my favorite things to do there is to simply stroll through the different sections and see what's new; there's always something fresh to discover. Whether you're an avid gardener or someone who just likes to be surrounded by beauty, Harry P. Leu Gardens offers something for everyone. And the best part? It's just a little slice of nature right in the middle of the city. You're only a few minutes away from the hustle and bustle, but it feels like you've entered another world entirely. If you're looking for a relaxing day surrounded by plants, flowers, and some of the most beautiful gardens you've ever seen, this place is definitely worth the visit.

Eco Tours and Wildlife Experiences: Paddle through Florida's Swamps

If you're really looking to connect with nature, you've got to experience an eco-tour or wildlife tour. These aren't your typical sightseeing tours, trust me. We're talking about real, up-close experiences with Florida's unique wildlife, all while paddling through some of the most beautiful, untouched swamps and waterways in the state.

One of the most amazing experiences I've had was paddling through the Black Hammock Adventures. It's just a short drive from downtown Orlando, and it's like stepping into another world. You hop into a kayak or canoe and glide across calm waters that are lined with lush cypress trees. The air smells earthy, fresh, and alive. And the wildlife? It's everywhere. You might see a manatee cruising by, or a heron perched on a branch, its sharp eyes scanning the waters below. And yes, there are alligators here, but don't let that scare you; this is their home, and you're just passing through. You're more likely to see them lounging in the sun or swimming in the distance, and it's honestly pretty magical to witness them in their natural habitat.

As you paddle, the guide will share fascinating facts about the swamp, the ecosystem, and the creatures that call it home. It's one thing to see alligators and birds in zoos, but when you're in their environment, in the heart of the swamp, it's a whole different experience. There's something humbling about seeing these creatures in the wild. It makes you appreciate the delicate balance of nature in a way you probably haven't before.

Even if you've never kayaked before, don't worry. These tours are designed for beginners, so you don't need to be a pro to have an amazing time. Just sit back, relax, and take in the sights, sounds, and smells of Florida's wild side. It's a truly immersive experience that leaves you feeling a little bit more connected to the natural world.

The Best Outdoor Adventure Parks in Orlando

Okay, let's get back to Orlando's adventure side. If you're craving a little more adrenaline, don't think that Orlando's all about theme parks and walking around. There are some incredible outdoor adventure parks where you can really stretch your legs and get your heart pumping.

One of the coolest places to check out is the **Orlando Tree Trek Adventure Park**. It's basically like being a kid again; except now you get to swing through trees on zip lines and conquer obstacle courses high

above the ground. Picture this: You're scaling rope bridges, ziplining through the air, and testing your balance as you make your way across suspended platforms. It's a thrill, and you get to enjoy the beauty of the forest from above. Whether you're with friends or family, this place is a blast, and it's definitely a workout too.

Another great spot for thrill-seekers is the **Boggy Creek Airboat Adventures**. If you've never been on an airboat before, you're in for a treat. You zoom across the waters at top speed, skimming over grasslands and winding through narrow swamp passages. You'll see all kinds of wildlife, from wild boar to bald eagles, and of course, more gators. It's exhilarating to feel the wind in your hair as you speed across the water, and it gives you a whole new appreciation for the swamps and wetlands around Orlando.

Lastly, if you're into hiking, you've got plenty of trails to explore. The **Black Bear Wilderness Loop Trail** is one of the best spots for a true wilderness experience. You'll hike through thick forests, past tranquil streams, and you might even catch a glimpse of a black bear or bobcat. It's the kind of place that makes you feel like you've escaped the city and entered another world entirely.

Orlando isn't just about theme parks; there's an entire world of outdoor adventure waiting to be discovered. Whether you're flying through trees on a zipline or paddling through quiet swamps, these natural experiences offer a whole new side to the city that you won't want to miss.

CHAPTER 8. ARTS AND CULTURE: DISCOVER ORLANDO'S CREATIVE SIDE

So, you've made your way to Orlando. Sure, everyone talks about the theme parks, and yeah, they're incredible. But what if I told you that Orlando's creative side is just as fascinating, with art, music, and performances waiting to be discovered all around the city? If you've got a thing for art, culture, and live performances, Orlando has more than enough to keep your curiosity buzzing.

Now, I know it's easy to think of Orlando as all about Mickey Mouse and roller coasters, but honestly, there's this whole other side to the city that's got a creative pulse running through it. And let me tell you, it's worth diving into.

I think the beauty of Orlando's arts scene is that it doesn't feel forced or like it's trying to be something it's not. It's real, it's exciting, and it's constantly evolving. Whether you're wandering down the streets, catching a Broadway show, or soaking in a piece of history, you'll see how this city is alive with artistic expression. So, let's talk about a few of the best spots where you can feel the creative energy, where every brushstroke, every note, every performance will make you feel like you're part of something bigger than just another tourist.

The Dr. Phillips Center for the Performing Arts: Broadway Shows and Concerts

Okay, picture this: you're sitting in an elegant, modern theater, the lights dimming as the anticipation in the room builds. Suddenly, the curtain rises, and you're swept into a world of drama, music, and breathtaking performances. That's the magic of the Dr. Phillips Center for the Performing Arts. If you're in Orlando and you've got even the slightest love for Broadway, live performances, or just the thrill of seeing something great on stage, this place is where you need to be.

Now, I won't lie to you; the Dr. Phillips Center isn't just a theater. It's an experience. It's where you'll see some of the best touring Broadway shows. I'm talking about everything from "Hamilton" to "The Lion King," and if you've ever dreamt of seeing a Broadway show but haven't made it to New York, this is as close as it gets. The sound, the lighting, the energy of the crowd; it all comes together to create this unforgettable vibe that only live theater can offer.

And it's not just about musicals. You'll also find concerts, symphonies, ballet performances, and so much more at the Dr. Phillips Center. If you're into classical music or even contemporary performances, there's always something amazing going on. The acoustics in the venue are spot on, making sure you get the best possible experience no matter what show you're seeing. Plus, the fact that it's located right in downtown Orlando means you can grab a bite to eat, soak in the city vibes, and then head to the theater to top off the night. It's pretty much a perfect evening.

Orlando Museum of Art: A Cultural Retreat

If you've got even a slight inclination toward visual arts, then you've got to check out the Orlando Museum of Art. It's one of those places that feels like it's been quietly influencing the city's cultural vibe for years, and it has so much more to offer than meets the eye. This place is an absolute gem, and trust me, you don't need to be a high-brow art lover to appreciate it.

The first thing you'll notice is the museum's commitment to showcasing local and regional artists. There's something special about walking through galleries that not only feature the work of established artists but also give a platform to those who are just starting out. You'll see a wide variety of styles; from contemporary pieces that make you think, to classical works that feel almost timeless. And what I love most is how the museum never feels overwhelming. The exhibits are well-curated, and there's always a new experience waiting around every corner.

One of the coolest things about the Orlando Museum of Art is that it's not just about hanging pictures on walls. It's about connecting with the audience, engaging in dialogue, and sparking conversations. There's usually some sort of event or artist talk happening, so you can get a deeper understanding of the works on display. Sometimes, they even host special workshops or interactive events, which I think adds such a personal touch to your visit.

Whether you're an art aficionado or just someone looking to enjoy an afternoon in a peaceful and inspiring space, the Orlando Museum of Art has something that'll make you think, reflect, and maybe even discover a new passion.

The Charles Hosmer Morse Museum of American Art: Iconic Tiffany Glass

Now, if you're a fan of intricate beauty, and I mean the kind that stops you in your tracks, the Charles Hosmer Morse Museum of American Art is where you need to head next. I'm talking about a museum dedicated to the incredible works of Louis Comfort Tiffany; yes, *that* Tiffany. And let me tell you, this place is a treasure trove of stunning stained glass, jewelry, and intricate art that feels like a work of magic rather than just craftsmanship.

The highlight, of course, is the Tiffany collection. You know those beautiful stained-glass windows you've seen in movies, the ones that make the light come alive in a way that feels almost spiritual? Yeah, this museum is home to some of the most iconic Tiffany glass works in the world. Walking through the museum feels like stepping into a dream world of vibrant colors and light, with every piece telling its own unique story. There's just something so mesmerizing about Tiffany's work; it's delicate, yet bold; timeless, yet fresh.

But it's not just about the glass. The museum also has a fascinating collection of American art from the 19th and 20th centuries. There are paintings, sculptures, and even decorative arts that transport you to different times and places. You'll leave this museum feeling inspired, reflective, and honestly, just in awe of the incredible talent that's been preserved here. It's one of those places that makes you pause and think about the beauty that's in the world, and it stays with you long after you've left.

Street Art and Murals: Explore Orlando's Urban Art Scene

Okay, if you're a fan of urban art, you're going to fall in love with Orlando's street art scene. There's something so raw and authentic about this type of art; it's like it's speaking directly to you, and you can't help but feel a connection to the creativity that's just bursting out of the walls. Orlando's urban art scene is a hidden treasure that not a lot of visitors know about, but trust me, you'll want to see it for yourself.

Take a stroll through the Milk District or even downtown, and you'll find entire walls covered in murals that reflect the soul of the city. There's so much life in these murals, so much energy. From vibrant colors to powerful messages, these works are a representation of Orlando's diverse culture, its history, and the people who call this city home. It's not just graffiti; it's art that demands to be noticed, art that tells stories.

What's so amazing about Orlando's street art scene is how accessible it is. It's not locked behind museum doors or hidden in galleries; it's right there on the streets, in plain sight, for everyone to see and enjoy. And because street art is constantly evolving, there's always something new to discover. Every time you walk through certain neighborhoods, you'll find a new piece of art, a new story, and a fresh burst of creativity.

Theatre and Live Performances: A Vibrant Local Culture

You know, one of the things I love most about Orlando is how alive the city feels with local culture, especially when it comes to theater and live performances. Sure, you can see big Broadway shows, but what about the local talent that's just waiting to surprise you with their amazing performances? That's one of Orlando's hidden gems.

The city has a thriving local theater scene, with multiple venues showcasing everything from comedies to dramas, and everything in between. Whether you're catching a show at the Orlando Shakespeare Theater, which puts on some seriously impressive productions, or you're at a smaller, more intimate venue watching a local troupe bring a story to life, there's something magical about being in the audience of a live performance. It's raw, it's real, and it's a reflection of the community. It's a culture that's constantly evolving, always pushing boundaries and challenging the norm.

What's cool about Orlando's local theater scene is that it really brings people together. The performances are often more interactive, and the energy in the room is something you just can't replicate with movies or TV. And who knows? You might just find yourself laughing so hard at a comedy show that your cheeks hurt, or so moved by a powerful drama that you can't stop thinking about it for days.

Orlando is not just about the big-name theme parks. The city's arts and culture scene is thriving, and whether you're into Broadway shows, world-class museums, street art, or intimate live performances, there's something here that'll captivate you. So, if you want to experience a side of Orlando that you can't find in a guidebook, look a little closer and discover the creative heart of this incredible city. Trust me, it'll leave you with memories that are just as lasting as the ones from the parks.

CHAPTER 9. DAY TRIPS FROM ORLANDO

Daytona Beach: A Coastal Escape

If you're in Orlando and looking for an escape to the coast, Daytona Beach is calling your name. Just a short drive away, it's the perfect spot to hit the sand, soak up the sun, and take a breather from all the excitement of the theme parks. There's something about the vibe of Daytona that feels like a whole different world. You've got the beach, the salty air, and the wide open spaces. It's one of those places where you can just breathe a little easier.

Imagine this: you're standing on the shoreline, toes buried in the warm sand, the sound of the waves crashing in front of you, and the breeze tousling your hair. It's the kind of place that makes you forget about everything for a while. And here's the thing: Daytona Beach isn't just about the sand and surf. There's a lot of history and culture tucked away here too. Whether you're into racing or history, Daytona's got you covered.

The Daytona International Speedway is one of the biggest draws. If you're a fan of NASCAR or just want to see where the magic happens, the speedway is definitely worth a visit. Even if you're not into racing, you'll be struck by the sheer scale of it all. It's like a monument to speed and excitement. And if you happen to be in town during a race weekend, well, get ready for a totally different level of energy. It's a huge part of Daytona's identity, and it adds a layer of excitement to the whole area.

But if you're looking for something a little more laid-back, Daytona Beach has that vibe too. Head over to the Daytona Beach Boardwalk for some classic beach town fun. You've got arcades, ice cream shops, and just a general sense of nostalgia. It's a place where you can walk around without a care in the world, grab some fried seafood, and watch the surfers do their thing. Daytona is the perfect mix of fun and relaxation.

It's one of those places where you can decide what kind of day you want to have. Whether you're out on the water, exploring the history of the area, or just chilling on the beach with a good book, Daytona Beach makes it easy to enjoy the simple things in life. Plus, it's so close to Orlando, you can easily get there in about an hour. If you need a break from all the theme park madness, Daytona's got the perfect laid-back coastal escape just waiting for you.

The Florida Everglades: Nature's Untamed Beauty

Alright, if you've got a little more time and a sense of adventure, let me tell you about the Florida Everglades. This place is *wild*. And I don't mean that in the "ooh, look, a cute little wildlife park" kind of way. No, the Everglades is a raw, untamed, and fiercely beautiful part of Florida that's worth exploring.

Here's the thing: the Everglades are one of those places that will make you feel like you're a million miles away from everything. You're surrounded by vast, open spaces and lush, swampy wetlands that go on forever.   It's   a   place

that forces you to slow down, breathe, and really take in what's around you. Picture it: giant cypress trees, vast grassy wetlands, and a sky so big it feels like it's going to swallow you up. It's peaceful, in its own wild way, but also kind of humbling.

And let's talk about the wildlife for a second. If you're someone who loves nature, the Everglades is like stepping into a different world. You've got alligators lounging in the sun, herons gliding over the water, and manatees floating by with that calm, effortless grace of theirs. There's something incredibly calming about watching these creatures in their natural habitat. But let's be real, there's also that sense of thrill knowing you're in the middle of a true wilderness. You never know what might be lurking just out of sight.

The best way to experience the Everglades? Get out on the water. Hop onto an airboat ride, and let me tell you, it's an experience you won't forget. The rush of wind in your face, the sound of the engine cutting through the water, and the sheer thrill of speeding across the vast swamp is unlike anything else. And as you zip through the water, you'll spot wildlife that you didn't even know existed; whether it's a lazy alligator sunbathing on the banks or a group of birds flying in formation above you.

You might think it's just a swamp, but it's so much more than that. The Everglades are one of the most unique ecosystems in the world, and getting the chance to experience it is truly humbling. It's a place that feels untouched by time, where nature reigns supreme and you're just a visitor, passing through on a brief adventure. If you're into something a little different, a little wild, and totally unforgettable, the Everglades should definitely be on your list.

St. Augustine: Historic Charm and Spanish Colonial Architecture

If you're someone who loves history and charm, then a day trip to St. Augustine is an absolute must. It's not far from Orlando, and let me tell you, this place will make you feel like you've stepped back in time. St. Augustine is the oldest continuously inhabited European-established settlement in the U.S., and the minute you step onto its cobblestone streets, you'll understand why it's so special.

What I love about St. Augustine is how it feels like a little piece of Europe tucked away in Florida. The Spanish colonial architecture is just gorgeous, with its narrow streets, pastel-colored buildings, and old-world charm. You'll find yourself wandering through historic sites that tell the story of a city that's been alive for centuries. There's something magical about being surrounded by so much history; like, you're walking in the footsteps of explorers, settlers, and pirates who made this place what it is today.

The Castillo de San Marcos is the crown jewel of St. Augustine. This 17th-century fort is one of the best-preserved in the country, and it's easy to see why it's such a big deal. The views from the top of the fort are incredible, and as you walk through the walls, you can almost hear the echoes of the past. It's not just a fort; it's a living, breathing piece of history. There's something deeply moving about standing in a place that's seen so much, from battles to peace treaties to quiet moments of reflection.

But St. Augustine isn't just about history; it's also about the little things that make a town feel alive. The shops here are full of quirky treasures, and the restaurants offer the kind of cozy atmosphere that makes you want to linger over a meal for hours. The St. Augustine Distillery is worth a visit if you're into craft spirits. And if you're a fan of ghosts or haunted places, well, St. Augustine has its fair share of spooky spots, too. The combination of history and charm, with a little bit of mystery thrown in, makes St. Augustine a place that's easy to fall in love with.

Miami: A Day Trip to the Magic City

Okay, if you're looking for something a little more fast-paced, vibrant, and full of life, then a day trip to Miami is going to blow your mind. Just a few hours south of Orlando, Miami is like a whole different world. The city has this energy that you can feel the second you arrive. It's the pulse of the music, the colors, the culture, and the people. Miami is a melting pot of everything that makes Florida unique, and it'll leave you with a whole new perspective on what the Sunshine State has to offer.

Miami is famous for its beaches, and when you see them for yourself, you'll get it. Picture this: pristine sand, turquoise waters, and the skyline of the city just off in the distance. Miami Beach is the place to be if you're in the mood to relax by the water, soak up some rays, and people-watch. But there's so much more to Miami than just the beach.

Little Havana is one of my favorite spots. It's like stepping into a vibrant, colorful slice of Cuba, right in the heart of Miami. The streets are lined with cigar shops, Cuban restaurants, and vibrant murals that bring the whole neighborhood to life. There's this infectious energy in the air, with the sound of salsa music and the smell of freshly brewed coffee filling the streets. Miami is all about culture, and Little Havana is the perfect example of that.

Then there's the art scene in Miami's Wynwood Walls. It's this open-air gallery where street art takes center stage. The murals are huge, colorful, and so full of life that they practically beg you to stop and take a photo. It's not just about seeing art; it's about feeling it, about experiencing the city through its visual language.

Miami isn't just a beach town; it's a cultural hub, a foodie's paradise, and a place that's constantly buzzing with energy. A day trip to Miami might be short, but it's definitely unforgettable. Whether you're soaking up the sun or exploring the city's neighborhoods, Miami will make you feel alive in a way that's hard to explain.

Clearwater Beach: A Perfect Getaway on the Gulf Coast

If you're looking for that perfect beach getaway, look no further than Clearwater Beach. It's just a few hours west of Orlando, and trust me, it's worth the drive. Clearwater Beach is exactly what you imagine when you think of a perfect Florida beach; soft, powdery sand, clear turquoise waters, and the kind of laid-back vibe that makes you feel like time slows down just for you.

Clearwater is the kind of place where you can relax and forget about everything else. Whether you're taking a walk down Pier 60, watching the street performers and musicians, or just lounging on the beach with a cold drink in hand, it's all about slowing down and enjoying the simple things. The sunsets here are incredible; seriously, you've never seen a sunset until you've seen one over the Gulf of Mexico.

But Clearwater isn't just about the beach. There's a whole bunch of other things to do if you want to mix it up. Head out on a dolphin-watching tour (trust me, seeing these beautiful creatures up close will take your breath away), or take a cruise to one of the nearby islands. You can also rent kayaks, paddleboards, or bikes to explore the area at your own pace.

It's the kind of place that's perfect for a quick getaway, whether you're looking to relax, explore, or just take in the natural beauty. Clearwater Beach is the ideal spot for anyone wanting a beach day that feels as dreamy as it sounds.

CHAPTER 10. HEALTH AND WELLNESS: TAKING CARE OF YOURSELF WHILE ON VACATION

Vacations are supposed to be an escape, right? A time to unwind, recharge, and leave behind the stress of everyday life. But let's be real: when you're on a trip, especially somewhere as exciting as Orlando, it's

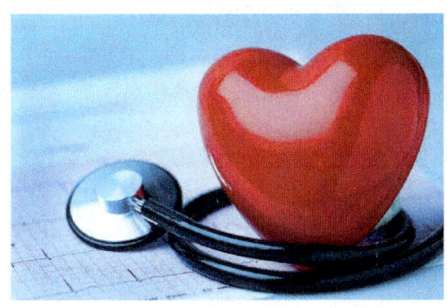

easy to get caught up in the whirlwind of theme parks, shopping, and endless activities. Before you know it, you've spent an entire day running from one attraction to the next, barely pausing for a breather. That's when you need to hit the reset button.

Taking care of yourself while you're on vacation isn't just about making sure you're having fun (although that's definitely part of it!). It's also about creating space for moments of relaxation and balance amidst all the excitement. Whether it's a quiet moment of reflection by the water, a spa day to treat your body right, or even just taking a slow walk through a garden, your wellness should be part of your Orlando adventure.

So, here's the deal: you're allowed to slow down. Seriously. Orlando's got more than just roller coasters and adrenaline-pumping rides; it's got a whole world of relaxation and rejuvenation waiting for you, and honestly,

taking a step back from the chaos can make the trip even more special. Think about it. You've planned this trip, you're here in one of the most dynamic cities in the world, and now it's time to enjoy it at your own pace.

And here's a secret; if you take time for yourself, the entire vacation feels like it lasts longer. You know how sometimes the days just blur together? That won't happen if you give yourself those moments of peace. Whether it's a morning walk before the crowds arrive or a gentle massage after a long day of exploring, you'll find that the little things add up and make a huge difference in how much you get out of your vacation.

Spa and Wellness Retreats in Orlando

Let's talk about spas. I mean, when was the last time you gave yourself permission to just unwind in peace? If you're heading to Orlando and haven't considered a spa day, let me tell you; you're missing out on an experience that could truly elevate your trip. Trust me, nothing beats the stress of travel like a deep tissue massage or a soothing facial, especially after a full day of theme park adventures.

One place that really stands out in Orlando is the *Waldorf Astoria Spa*. Picture this: you're surrounded by calming music, the scent of essential oils floating through the air, and a team of experts ready to make your body feel like new. Whether you're booking a hot stone massage to work out those tired muscles or a calming aromatherapy session to clear your mind, this spa knows how to give you the ultimate relaxation experience. And here's the best part: it's not just about getting pampered; it's about giving yourself the gift of time. Imagine slipping away from all the excitement for just a few hours, and letting go of every worry that's been building up.

If you're in the mood for something a bit more holistic, the *Miracle Mile*  *Spa* is another gem. This place has a more organic, healing vibe to it. It's the kind of spot where you can enjoy things like reiki healing or energy massages, which are perfect for getting in touch with your inner self. After all, wellness isn't just about physical relaxation; it's also about restoring your mind, and Miracle Mile gives you the space to do exactly that.

But Orlando isn't just about high-end spa experiences. You can find more accessible options, too. Some hotels offer their own wellness services, like aromatherapy massages or yoga sessions right on the property. A lot of resorts have those special packages that let you pamper yourself without leaving the grounds. So, whether you're looking for something extravagant or just a simple, chill vibe, Orlando's wellness scene has something for you.

Yoga and Fitness Studios for a Healthy Vacation

Now, let's talk about staying active. You know how after a few days of travel, you start feeling a little... off? Your body needs to stretch, move, and just find its groove again. But the great thing is that Orlando has a pretty amazing variety of yoga and fitness options that will help you stay in tune with your body without having to sacrifice your vacation vibes.

If yoga is your thing, I can't recommend *The Yoga Studio* enough. It's one of those places that feels like a sanctuary. Whether you're a seasoned yogi or just getting started, this studio offers classes that will help you reset your body and mind. The best part? They offer classes for all skill levels, so whether you want a gentle stretch or a more intense flow, you can find exactly what you need. Imagine waking up early, slipping into your favorite comfy clothes, and heading to a morning class that'll leave you feeling centered and calm. It's one of those things that makes you feel like you're taking care of yourself in all the right ways. Plus, many of their sessions focus on mindfulness, which is perfect for slowing down the pace of your busy Orlando trip.

And if you're into fitness but prefer a different kind of workout, places like *Orlando Strength* and *CycleBar* have you covered. These places aren't just gyms; they're communities. You'll find people who are passionate about movement, and the energy is contagious. I get it, after a long day of park hopping, it might be the last thing on your mind to hit the gym. But I promise, once you make it part of your routine, it's a game changer. You'll feel stronger, more energized, and maybe even a little more connected to your surroundings. Plus, you'll be guilt-free when you indulge in that extra churro at the theme park!

Relaxation Spots for Stress-Free Days

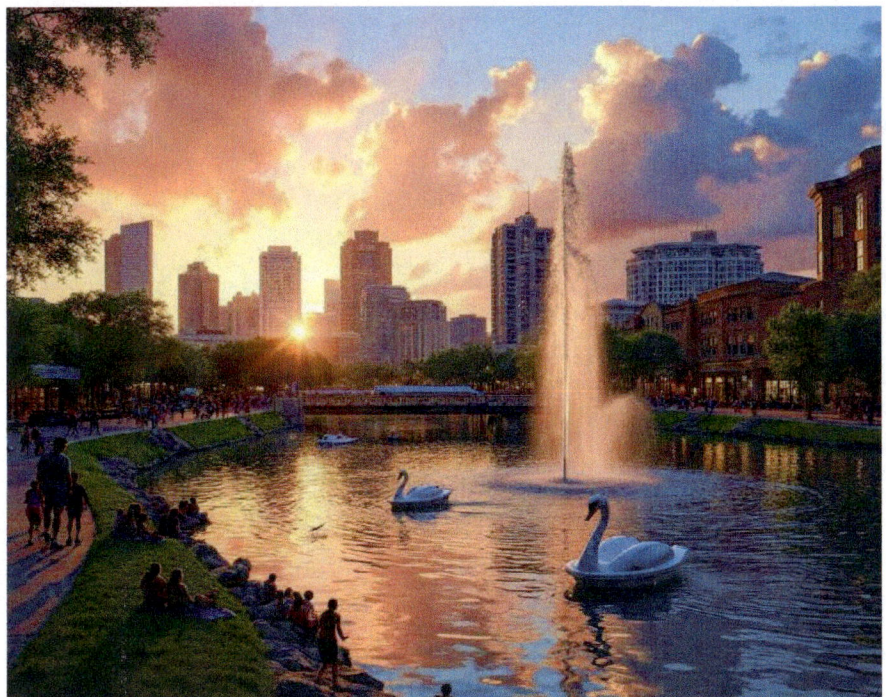

Sometimes, the best thing you can do for your well-being is to *not* do anything at all. Orlando is full of hidden gems where you can simply chill out and enjoy the peace. One of my favorite spots is *Lake Eola Park*. It's a beautiful, serene place right in the middle of downtown, and it's perfect for just zoning out for a bit. The sound of the water, the swans gliding across the lake, and the quiet energy of the park create an atmosphere where time seems to slow down. It's the kind of place where you can go for a walk, sit on a bench with a book, or just people-watch. And, if you're feeling a little extra, you can even rent a paddle boat and take a spin on the lake.

Then there's the *Leu Gardens*, which is another peaceful escape. It's like stepping into a different world where everything moves at its own pace. The gardens are meticulously cared for, and you'll find yourself wandering through paths filled with lush greenery, vibrant flowers, and tranquil ponds. It's the perfect place to clear your mind, breathe deeply, and just exist in the present moment.

But maybe you're someone who finds relaxation through art and culture. If that's you, head over to the *Orlando Museum of Art*. The quiet, contemplative vibe of the museum is perfect for a slow afternoon, and you'll find that the art exhibits give you plenty to reflect on. It's a great place to just unwind and let your mind wander without any pressure.

Healthy Eating in Orlando: Fresh, Local, and Delicious

Orlando's food scene is so much more than theme park snacks (though I'll admit, the churros are hard to resist). If you're looking for healthy, delicious meals that fuel your body while still making your taste buds dance, you're in the right place. Orlando's food scene has exploded with fresh, local, and seasonal dishes that are perfect for keeping you energized and feeling good.

One place that's always on my radar when I'm in town is *The Glass Knife*. It's this beautiful café that serves up fresh pastries, breakfast bowls, and lunch options; all with a focus on using high-quality ingredients. Whether you're craving something light like a fresh smoothie bowl or a hearty grain bowl packed with veggies, The Glass Knife nails it every time. It's a cozy spot that feels like a treat but without all the heaviness that comes with some indulgent vacation meals.

If you're in the mood for something even more fresh and farm-to-table, *Farm & Haus* is the way to go. This local gem serves up healthy comfort food made from locally sourced ingredients. They've got everything from avocado toast to organic chicken and quinoa bowls that will make you feel like you're getting the nourishment you need while still treating yourself to something tasty.

And don't even get me started on *Seasons 52*. This place is all about seasonal dishes made with fresh, light ingredients that make you feel good about what you're eating. You can enjoy a delicious meal without the guilt; think grilled seafood, roasted veggies, and the kind of flavors that make you want to come back again and again.

Orlando really has become a haven for anyone looking to eat clean without sacrificing flavor. From farmer's markets to healthy restaurants, the options are endless, and they all focus on making sure you're fueling your body with what it needs to thrive during your vacation. So go ahead; try something new, indulge in a fresh, healthy dish, and feel great doing it.

CHAPTER 11. ORLANDO FOR SPECIAL OCCASIONS

Alright, let's talk about romance. Picture this: you and your significant other, in the heart of Orlando, creating memories that will last a lifetime. A honeymoon in Orlando isn't just about going on rides or taking in the theme parks; though trust me, there's plenty of that; it's about finding those moments that feel like you're in your own world, just the two of you.

Maybe you're waking up in a cozy resort room with a stunning view of the parks or the lake, knowing that the day ahead is filled with nothing but adventure, laughter, and a little bit of magic. Imagine strolling down the streets of Disney Springs, hand-in-hand, the lights twinkling around you as you both enjoy a leisurely dinner by the water. It's the kind of romantic atmosphere that feels straight out of a fairy tale.

And speaking of fairy tales; how could we talk about Orlando without mentioning the sheer romance that is Walt Disney World? Yeah, I know, it might sound a bit cliché, but trust me when I say that there's something so special about experiencing Disney as a couple. Maybe it's the charming little shops in the parks, the quiet boat rides, or the parades that make you feel like you're in a dream. Or maybe it's the way your hearts beat faster when you're on Space Mountain, screaming together and sharing that exhilarating rush. Either way, Orlando knows how to make a honeymoon unforgettable, even in the most unexpected places.

But here's the thing: while the theme parks are a huge draw, Orlando has so much more to offer for couples looking for that perfect romantic getaway. Take a day trip to the Kennedy Space Center and stand hand-in-hand beneath the giant rockets, exploring the vastness of space. The experience is humbling, awe-inspiring, and incredibly romantic in a way you wouldn't expect.

Then there are the quieter spots in Orlando, those hidden gems that let you relax and savor the moment. The serene beauty of Lake Eola Park is perfect for a picnic, or maybe even a quiet boat ride. Renting a swan boat and paddling around together? It's one of those little moments you'll remember forever.

For dinner, there's no shortage of romantic dining options. You've got places like California Grill at Disney's Contemporary Resort, with a breathtaking view of the Magic Kingdom fireworks. It's a beautiful spot to watch the sun set over the park, enjoying a gourmet meal with your favorite person.

So yeah, Orlando isn't just for families or thrill-seekers; it's for the hopeless romantics, too. There's so much about this city that makes it feel like you've stepped into your own romantic adventure. Whether you're celebrating the start of your married life, or simply looking to reconnect, Orlando knows how to set the stage for romance.

Planning a Family Reunion in Orlando: Where to Stay and What to Do

Okay, let's dive into the whole family reunion thing. First off, Orlando? Total winner for family reunions. I mean, who doesn't want to spend a few days in a place that's all about making memories? And when you've got a large group to entertain, Orlando has something for everyone; from the tiniest toddler to your aunt who still insists she's too old for roller coasters but secretly loves them.

So, let's talk accommodations first. You've got your family-friendly resorts and hotels, which are pretty much designed for this kind of trip. I mean, think about it: places with pools big enough for everyone to swim together, suites that can fit a crowd, and all kinds of activities to keep everyone entertained when you're not hitting the parks. A great spot for this is the Walt Disney World Resort, where you'll find villas that can accommodate large groups with ease. And let's be real; how amazing would it be to have your family right in the heart of all the magic?

But if you're looking for something a little more laid-back, there are plenty of vacation homes and villas in Orlando that are just perfect for a family reunion. These homes are big enough to fit everyone comfortably, and the best part? You get your own space to spread out and bond, plus you've got all the comforts of home; kitchens for family dinners, BBQs, private pools, and game rooms. It's like you're hosting a family reunion in your own little Orlando paradise.

Now, what about things to do once you've got your accommodations sorted? You're in luck because Orlando is bursting with family-friendly activities. First off, theme parks. You can't really go wrong here. Walt Disney World is an obvious choice, and it's got something for every age. If your family's into more thrills, Universal Studios and Islands of Adventure are great options for the adrenaline junkies in the group. And the best part? Most of these places offer group discounts, which means you can save some cash while making memories that'll last a lifetime.

But let's not forget about the other cool things Orlando has to offer. You can take the whole crew to the Crayola Experience, where kids and adults alike can let their creativity run wild. Or spend the day at Gatorland, where you can get up close with alligators, feed them, and even watch crazy shows that'll have your family laughing for hours. And if you're looking for something a little quieter, a trip to Lake Eola Park for a picnic or a boat ride is perfect for bonding and just soaking up the Orlando sunshine.

In the evenings, head over to Disney Springs for dinner, shopping, and entertainment. There's something about walking through the lively streets with your family, grabbing ice cream, and watching live music that just feels magical.

And when you all gather together at the end of the day to relax, whether you're playing board games in the living room or sitting around the pool with a drink in hand, those moments of connection? They're what make family reunions truly special. Orlando gives you all the space to bond, laugh, and create stories that will be told for years to come.

Orlando for Anniversaries and Celebrations: Special Packages and Deals

Celebrating an anniversary or any special occasion in Orlando? Well, buckle up because this city knows how to make things feel special. Whether you're celebrating a milestone anniversary, a birthday, or just the fact that you survived another year together (hey, that counts too), Orlando is a place where you can turn any celebration into something memorable.

Let's start with the obvious; Walt Disney World. Sure, it might be known for kids and families, but did you know they also offer special anniversary packages? Imagine walking down Main Street at Magic Kingdom, hand in hand with your partner, and seeing your names on a cute little celebration button. It's small, but it's those little touches that make Orlando stand out. And if you want to go all out, there are private tours, VIP experiences, and even fireworks cruises that'll give you a celebration like no other.

But hey, if Disney isn't your vibe, Orlando still has plenty of ways to make your anniversary unforgettable. Check out the luxurious resorts and spas that offer romantic packages, complete with couples massages, gourmet meals, and champagne to toast your love. You could even book a hot air balloon ride for a once-in-a-lifetime experience that'll leave you both breathless; literally and figuratively. The feeling of floating above the city, with the Orlando skyline in the distance and nothing but the sound of the breeze? It's incredibly romantic.

And let's not forget about dining. Orlando is home to some seriously amazing restaurants that will make your anniversary feel extra special. Think about a candlelit dinner overlooking the water at The Boathouse in Disney Springs, or a chic rooftop meal at The Edison. These are the kind of places where the ambiance, food, and service come together to make you feel like you're the only two people in the world.

If you want something a little less traditional but still super memorable, book a private yacht tour or a dinner cruise. There's something about being out on the water with your loved one, the skyline lighting up around you as you share a delicious meal and toast to the years you've spent together.

Orlando's not just for families and honeymooners; it's a place where love is celebrated in all its forms, and every anniversary or special occasion can feel like a fairy tale. From VIP experiences to romantic dinners, this city has a way of making every moment feel a little more magical.

CHAPTER 12. SAFETY TIPS AND TRAVEL ADVICE

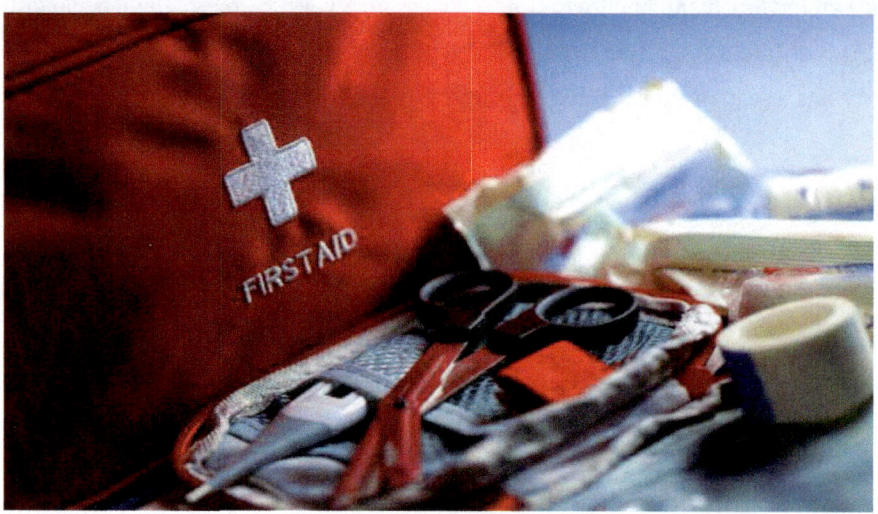

Staying Safe While Exploring Orlando

Alright, let's talk about something we all want to avoid but still need to be prepared for; staying safe while you're out and about in Orlando. Look, Orlando is an amazing place, filled with fun and excitement, but like any city, it's always good to keep your wits about you, especially when you're in unfamiliar surroundings.

First things first, safety is all about awareness. It sounds simple, but it can make a huge difference. When you're in the hustle and bustle of theme parks or even just out shopping on International Drive, it's easy to get caught up in the moment and lose track of what's going on around you. Trust me, I get it. You're excited, you're having fun, and you're here to make the most of your trip. But sometimes, a little bit of mindfulness can go a long way.

When you're walking around, especially in crowded areas, try to keep your personal items close. That backpack you're carrying with all your essentials? Keep it in front of you, not behind. If you're using a cross body bag, make sure it's always securely closed. Pickpocketing is rare in Orlando, but that doesn't mean you can't be a little proactive about your belongings. The same goes for your phone; don't leave it lying around while you're eating at a restaurant or waiting for a ride. A quick grab-and-go moment could ruin your whole day.

Orlando's also a city that's constantly buzzing, especially at night. If you're heading out to a bar or a late-night event, just be aware of your surroundings. Stick to well-lit areas and avoid walking alone in unfamiliar parts of the city after dark. I know, it sounds like common sense, but sometimes it's easy to forget when you're having the time of your life. So, whether you're in the theme parks or exploring downtown, keeping a general sense of awareness will help ensure your trip stays fun and safe.

But, hey, Orlando is a pretty friendly city overall. People are usually really nice, and most tourists are just as excited as you to be here. So don't be afraid to ask someone for directions or help if you need it. The locals have a pretty good grasp on where to go and what to do, and they'll be happy to point you in the right direction.

Emergency Contacts and Healthcare Services in Orlando

Now, let's talk about something that, while we hope you never need to use, is something you should still be prepared for: emergency contacts and healthcare. The good news? Orlando is pretty well-equipped for any situation that might arise, and knowing where to turn in case of an emergency can give you peace of mind so you can enjoy your trip without worry.

First things first: if you need emergency services, dialing **911** in the US will get you right to the people who can help, whether it's for a medical emergency, fire, or police. But in case of medical needs, it's good to know where the nearest hospitals or urgent care centers are. You never want to be caught off guard. Here are a few spots you should keep in mind:

- **Orlando Health – Orlando Regional Medical Center**: This is one of the main hospitals in the city and is located close to downtown Orlando. If you're in the area and need immediate care, this is a top-notch place to go.
- **AdventHealth Orlando**: Another excellent healthcare option, located near the theme park area. It's a little closer to the major resorts and tourist spots, so it's easy to get to if you're staying near Disney or Universal.

- **Urgent Care Centers**: For minor injuries, illness, or just feeling under the weather, Orlando has a variety of urgent care centers, and they're dotted throughout the city. You don't have to travel far to find one, and they'll get you taken care of quickly without the hassle of an ER visit.

Also, a quick tip: many theme parks and resorts have on-site first aid stations. So if something minor happens; let's say you get a little too sunburned or sprain your ankle from walking too much; there's no need to panic. Just head to one of these spots, and they'll take care of you.

But let's be real; healthcare doesn't just stop at emergency situations. If you need a pharmacy or over-the-counter medicine, you'll find plenty of Walgreens and CVS locations all over Orlando. You're never far from a place where you can grab some aspirin, sunscreen, or any other essentials you might need to feel better.

Orlando Travel Insurance: Why It's Worth It

You're probably thinking, "Why do I need travel insurance for a vacation to Orlando?" Well, it's one of those things you hope you never need to use, but it's incredibly valuable if something goes wrong. Life happens, right? Flights get delayed, luggage gets lost, or you might fall ill right before your trip. Travel insurance can step in and save you from some of the headache that could otherwise derail your fun.

Think about it: Orlando's a place where you're constantly on the move. Whether you're at a theme park, dining at a new restaurant, or sightseeing, you're always going from one activity to the next. And in a city that's as action-packed as Orlando, a little extra protection can go a long way. For instance, if you get sick and need to cancel your plans, travel insurance could help reimburse your non-refundable expenses. It might also cover medical expenses if you get injured during your trip. Sure, it's an extra cost, but the peace of mind knowing you've got it can be priceless.

Plus, if you're heading out of the country to get to Orlando, travel insurance can cover things like lost luggage or emergency evacuation if something goes wrong. Again, it's one of those things you hope you never have to use, but in case you do, it'll make everything a lot less stressful.

The best part? Travel insurance doesn't have to be expensive. There are plenty of affordable options out there that fit a wide range of needs.

Before you book your flights, consider adding a little extra security to your trip by looking into travel insurance. It'll be one less thing to worry about when you're exploring everything Orlando has to offer.

Tips for Keeping Your Valuables Safe

Alright, we've covered the big safety stuff; emergencies, healthcare, and insurance; but there's another layer of security that's just as important when you're traveling: keeping your valuables safe. No one wants to think about losing their wallet, phone, or passport, but it's always smart to be prepared.

Let's start with your phone. It's probably the most important thing you'll carry with you during your trip, and it's also the easiest to lose track of. Whether you're checking out a theme park, walking around downtown Orlando, or grabbing lunch, it's a good idea to keep your phone in a secure pocket or in a bag that you can keep a close eye on. A small, anti-theft backpack or a crossbody bag with zippers can help keep things secure while also giving you easy access when you need it.

And speaking of bags; don't leave your stuff unattended. I get it; you're excited, and maybe you want to grab a snack or check out the gift shop for a souvenir. But always, always keep your belongings within arm's reach. Even when you're sitting down to rest, don't leave your bag behind on the chair. It might feel like you're the only one in the world, but you'd be surprised at how quickly someone can take advantage of an unattended bag.

For things like your wallet, passport, or important documents, I recommend using a money belt or hidden pouch that you can wear under your clothes. It sounds a little old-school, but it's seriously one of the safest ways to keep everything secure. There are also anti-theft wallets that have RFID-blocking technology, which is great for preventing digital theft. It's one of those things you might not think about, but in the crowded areas of theme parks or busy shopping districts, it's better to be safe than sorry.

And lastly, be careful with your valuables at night. Orlando is a pretty safe city, but like any place, it's always a good idea to use caution when you're walking around after dark. Stick to well-lit areas, and if you're heading back to your hotel after an evening event, make sure you're not wandering through any unfamiliar or poorly lit streets.

Look, keeping your valuables safe isn't about paranoia; it's about being smart and prepared. By staying aware and taking small precautions, you can avoid the stress of losing your things and focus on enjoying everything Orlando has to offer. Trust me, you'll want to spend your time making memories, not dealing with a lost phone or wallet.

CONCLUSION

Making the Most of Your Orlando Holiday

Okay, let's take a step back for a second and reflect on what this whole Orlando adventure is all about. I mean, you're here for one thing; to have an unforgettable time, right? And Orlando is that perfect place where every day can feel like the best day of your life. Whether you're zooming down a rollercoaster at Universal, soaking in the magic at Disney, or simply wandering around exploring the countless hidden gems in the city, there's always something new to experience.

The trick to making the most of your Orlando holiday isn't about cramming every single ride, show, or restaurant into your itinerary. I know it's tempting; especially when you see how much there is to do. But sometimes the best moments happen when you slow down a little. Don't forget to take in the small things, like watching a sunset by Lake Eola, trying a new snack, or just enjoying a quiet moment with friends and family after a long day at the parks. Those moments are the ones that often stick with you the longest.

And if you're anything like me, you know that vacations are about more than just sightseeing. It's about creating memories, having new experiences, and soaking in everything that makes a place special. So while you're here, remember that it's not just about getting through the must-see lists; it's about embracing everything Orlando has to offer, from the hustle of the theme parks to the peaceful charm of the quiet streets.

Don't stress over the perfect plan. Be flexible. Be open to spontaneous adventures. If you miss a ride, there's no need to freak out. Trust me, you'll find something just as exciting in the next spot you visit. Keep your heart and mind open to the city, and you'll end up discovering the parts of Orlando that only the lucky few ever get to experience. And those are the moments that make a trip truly unforgettable.

Final Tips for an Unforgettable Vacation Experience

Now, I've given you a ton of info already, but here are a few final tips to help you really make your Orlando vacation something special. Let's keep it simple and fun:

- **Get there early**: If you're planning to visit the big theme parks, trust me, early mornings are your best friend. Not only will you beat the crowds, but you'll also get a chance to experience the parks when they're not at their busiest. Plus, there's something magical about seeing the sunrise over Magic Kingdom or Universal Studios before the park fills up.
- **Don't over-schedule**: It can be tempting to jam-pack your days with activities, but sometimes the best days are the ones that aren't as planned. If you're tired, take a break and wander around a quieter part of the city. You might find a cute café, a quiet park,

or an off-the-beaten-path museum you hadn't even thought of. Don't be afraid to go with the flow!

- **Be kind to yourself**: Look, we all get caught up in trying to do it all, and sometimes things don't go as planned. Maybe it's raining, or maybe that one ride you really wanted to go on is closed. It's all part of the journey. Take a deep breath, laugh it off, and go find something else that'll make your day special. Flexibility is key!

- **Capture the moments**: You don't have to document every single second, but take time to capture those memories. Whether it's a photo of you and your family standing in front of Cinderella's Castle or a candid shot of you laughing with friends at a theme park, those pictures will be treasures long after you've left Orlando. Just don't get too caught up in the camera; sometimes the best memories are the ones you experience with your eyes, not your phone.

- **Indulge in the food**: Seriously, Orlando's food scene is an experience on its own. From theme park snacks (hello, churros and giant turkey legs!) to upscale dining at Disney Springs, there's something for every taste. Don't rush through meals just to get to the next ride. Take your time, savor the flavors, and enjoy some downtime while you recharge.

- **Don't forget to relax**: This is your vacation, after all. Orlando is a city that's constantly moving and offering up new things to do, but remember to slow down when you need to. Take a break at the pool, or find a quiet bench in a park and just people-watch.

Sometimes, the best moments come from stepping back and breathing in the energy of the city.

Looking Ahead: Why You'll Want to Visit Orlando Again

So, as your trip winds down, you might start to think about what's next. And here's the thing about Orlando: once you've been here, it has this way of pulling you back. There's something about this city that sticks with you, like it leaves an imprint on your soul. The magic isn't just in the theme parks, but in the experiences that unfold throughout your stay. Every visit feels like it has the potential to be a little different from the last, no matter how many times you come back.

Maybe next time you'll try out some of the attractions you missed this time. Or maybe you'll revisit your favorite rides, reliving the joy they brought you. And don't even get me started on the seasonal events; Halloween at Universal, Christmas at Disney World, or Mardi Gras at SeaWorld. Orlando is always changing, offering something fresh and exciting every time you visit.

But more than the attractions, Orlando offers you a chance to unwind, reflect, and make connections. It's a city where families reconnect, friends make lasting memories, and even solo travelers find moments of quiet joy in unexpected places. And that's why you'll want to come back. There's no place quite like it.

I'm not saying you have to come back next week, but I'd be willing to bet that Orlando will stay on your radar for years to come. And when it calls you back, you'll be ready to dive into the magic again, knowing that there's always something new to discover, something more to enjoy.

So go ahead, enjoy every single moment of your Orlando trip. Don't rush it, don't overthink it; just live it. And when you leave, take a little piece of that magic with you. Trust me, you'll be counting down the days until your next visit, and when you return, Orlando will be waiting with open arms, ready to give you even more memories to cherish.

Printed in Dunstable, United Kingdom

66785836R00087